Adva
LIBERATING P

MW01283696

"As with so many of her earlier splendid contributions to theological research, Sister Gloria Schaab, SSJ makes an important contribution with *Liberating Pneumatologies*. The text is characterized by a thoroughly systematic approach that is careful, balanced, thoughtful, intellectually challenging, and highly readable. I particularly appreciated the distinction Schaab honors in her work between the "classical" and the "contextual" approaches to systematic theology, giving each its due in the history of the development of the doctrine of the Holy Spirit. I deeply appreciated Schaab's own working definition of the Holy Spirit as the One who "liberates human persons *from* those experiences that oppress in mind, body, and spirit and *for* a radical sense of mission that carries forward into the reign of God". Finally, I was particularly impressed by the last chapter, in which Schaab explores the implications of a renewed pneumatology that takes seriously the ecological and cosmological framework that characterizes postmodernity. I appreciated her emphasis on the urgency of continuing to develop a theology freed from Western philosophical dualism, from the notion that spirit and matter are opposed to one another and toward "an embodied doctrine of God [as] signaled by the inaugural hymn of Genesis where the Creator Spirit (ruah) breathes the world into existence and thereby enfleshes itself in the creation and maintenance of the natural order". Theologians and students alike are in Schaab's debt for this fine contribution."

—*Father Dave Gentry-Akin, Professor of Theology*
Saint Mary's College of California

"With her customary combination of scholarly acumen and pastoral sensitivity, Professor Schaab has provided a clearly written, well researched, and accessible volume that provides historical insight into Christian understanding of the Holy Spirit while challenging readers to discover the Spirit in the particularities of contemporary communities of faith. Attuned to experiences of suffering and exclusion as well as culturally mediated experiences of the divine, Schaab inspires readers to recognize liberating and healing modes of relationship as the movement of the Holy Spirit in their own lives."

—*Elena Procario-Foley, Ph.D.*
Br. John G. Driscoll Professor of Jewish-Catholic Studies, Iona College

"An engaging and well-structured book! At once wide-ranging and tightly focused, it spans the centuries like a detective looking for clues about the liberating character and action of the Holy Spirit. With clarity and grace the author finds these clues from scripture to contemporary theology, and weaves them together into a source of inspiration and learning. A terrific text for the classroom."

—*Elizabeth A. Johnson, CSJ*
Distinguished Professor Emerita, Fordham University

"Framed by the key insight that each act of the Spirit is personally, socio-politically, and theologically liberating, this volume presents a masterful exploration of the Person, agency, and activity of the Holy Spirit. What makes Schaab's work stand out is its rigorous harvest of the insights of generations of theologians who have given serious thought to the actions of the Spirit in their own time and historical context. Here, the scholarship of women, African American, and Latinx theologians stands shoulder-to-shoulder with the influential insights of classical theology. As a result, Schaab makes a vital and comprehensive contribution to the study of the Holy Spirit."

—*Jorge Presmanes, OP, Professor of Theology,*
Director of the Institute for Hispanic/Latino Theology and Ministry
Barry University, Miami, Florida

LIBERATING
PNEUMATOLOGIES

LIBERATING
PNEUMATOLOGIES

Spirit Set Free

GLORIA L. SCHAAB

A HERDER & HERDER BOOK
THE CROSSROAD PUBLISHING COMPANY
NEW YORK

A Herder & Herder Book
The Crossroad Publishing Company www.crossroadpublishing.com

The text of this book is set in 12/14 Filosofia.

Composition and cover design by Sophie Appel
Cover artwork, 'Orange Energy Field' (detail), by Margie Thompson, SSJ

Library of Congress Cataloging-in-Publication Data
available upon request from the Library of Congress.
ISBN 978-0-8245-9501-2 paperback
ISBN 978-0-8245-0528-8 ePub
ISBN 978-0-8245-0545-5 mobi

Books published by The Crossroad Publishing Company may be purchased at special quantity discount rates for classes and institutional use. For information, please e-mail sales@crossroadpublishing.com.

To our religious Congregation —
The Sisters of Saint Joseph of Philadelphia
May the Spirit forever liberate us to a radical sense of mission!

CONTENTS

ACKNOWLEDGMENTS

IT IS OFTEN SAID by many authors that completion of a project of this kind cannot be accomplished alone, and it is no less true in this case. Writing in the midst of the COVID-19 pandemic, during a shift in teaching and administration from in-person to remote, and between seemingly innumerable Zoom meetings, only amplified my gratitude for the generosity of those whom I wish to acknowledge. Their unstinting support set my spirit free to engage fully in this project.

- Chris Myers of Crossroad Publishing, whose good will, patience, and encouragement smoothed the course of this project, and Julie Boddorf, who skillfully facilitated the production process.
- Margie Thompson, SSJ, dear friend, sister religious, and first reader of all my manuscripts, whose appraisal, feedback, and excitement about this project buoyed my creative energies.
- The Sisters of Saint Joseph of Divine Shepherd Convent—Trina Fee, Mary Ethel Haeberlin, and Margie Thompson—whose hospitality, graciousness, and thoughtfulness provided a welcoming space for me in the final stretch of this effort.
- Jorge Presmanes, OP, and James Nickoloff, friends and colleagues in theology at Barry University, who pointed me to valuable resources for the chapters on Latinx and Latin American pneumatologies.
- Karen Callaghan, Dean of the College of Arts and Sciences at Barry University, whose consideration, encouragement, and good sense aided the completion of this manuscript.

May Spirit who is gift, who is love, who is relationship, who is liberation rise up within you and companion you always!

Gloria L. Schaab, SSJ
Easter 2021

W HAT MIGHT ONE EXPECT from the Holy Spirit set free?
What might one expect of the Holy Spirit *as* God?
What might one expect of the Holy Spirit in the fullness
of Personhood,
equal in Divinity, unique in Identity?
Not simply the Spirit "of"—of God, of the Father, of the Son, of Jesus—
but *as God*?

What might one expect of the Holy Spirit set free from prepositional limitation, unfettered by ecclesiological structures?

No less than the unexpected, the serendipitous, the surprising, the
liberative.

An intuition stimulated the creation of this manuscript. Two aspects
of this intuition are suggested by its title, which, in fact, preceded any
research. Since "to ask, 'Who is God?' is to focus on what [God] is
doing,"[1] this text first reflects my conviction, born of experience, study,
and reflection, that *each genuine act of the Holy Spirit is essentially liberating*—personally, communally, socially, politically, ecclesially, and theologically. While other effects may accompany this experience, liberation
emerges as the heart of the encounter. It is this intuition that became
the hermeneutic guiding the research and organization of this work. To
my surprise and delight, the research itself confirmed my initial insight.

Nonetheless, the process of the text took on a life of its own, calling
me to be responsive to the prompting of the Spirit through the discovery, sifting, and selection of those theologians whose work would
be included in this book. Despite the frequent refrain concerning the
paucity of attention paid to pneumatology in the discipline, a review
of literature over the past fifty years reveals that pneumatology is an
idea whose time has come. "Within living memory," writes Patrick

---

1   James Cone, *A Black Theology of Liberation* (New York: Lippincott, 1970), 142.

Corcoran, "there has been no period...when the Holy Spirit has been so much in the public eye. He has become a superstar—one whose musical has not yet been written—but nonetheless a superstar."[2] However, while writings on the Holy Spirit are manifold, systematically developed pneumatologies are not. This proved to be both blessing and challenge. The blessing has been discovering unexpected, creative, and thought-provoking insights from theologians unfamiliar to me; the challenge has been in uncovering them among the abundance.

Second, this text is intentionally a *pneumatology*, a systematic theology of the distinctive Person, agency, and activity of the Holy Spirit from both classical and contextual perspectives. Although the insights of pneumatology cannot, should not, and need not be divorced from personal prayer and discernment and can be spiritually liberating, this text is deliberate in its focus on the theological, not the spiritual. "We need to distinguish," states Samuel Soliván, "between the Spirit as person and [as] the attribute of spirituality. There are as many spiritualities as there are spirits.... The Holy Spirit is more than a divine attribute of spirituality."[3] Hence, while the questions for reflection at the end of each chapter seek to tease out some of the spiritual dimensions and implications of the pneumatology presented, this is *not* a work of spirituality.

Moreover, this is explicitly *not* a work of ecclesiology or Christology. While the Holy Spirit is indispensable to the formation of the Church community and to the mission and ministry of Jesus, too often the Person and agency of the Spirit are subsumed or overshadowed in such frameworks. To identify and highlight the particularity of the Holy Spirit, therefore, this text lifts up imagery reflecting a variety of liberating experiences specifically attributed to the agency of the Holy Spirit. By no means exhaustive, the imagery selected represents the perspectives of a broad array of theologians who write from both classical and contextual perspectives. While pneumatology cannot, should not, and need not be

---

2   Patrick Corcoran, C.M., "The Holy Spirit and the Life of the Spirit Today,"
     Proceedings of the Irish Biblical Association 3 (1979): 97.

3   Samuel Soliván, "The Holy Spirit—Personalization and the Affirmation of
     Diversity: A Pentecostal Hispanic Perspective," in *Teología en Conjunto: A
     Collaborative Hispanic Protestant Theology*, ed. José David Rodríguez and Loida I.
     Martell-Otero (Louisville: Westminster John Knox Press, 1997), 54.

divorced from ecclesiology and Christology, this text makes every effort to emphasize the distinctive presence and agency of the Holy Spirit encountered in individual, social, and cultural events and experiences.

Chapter One sets the parameters of this project by squarely focusing on the Personhood of the Holy Spirit. After a brief overview of the imagery of the Holy Spirit in the Scriptures, it raises up the distinct Person of the Holy Spirit, focusing on the Gospels (most specifically of John) and on Acts and the Epistles. In addition to affirming the Personhood of the Spirit, demonstrated throughout the Scriptures is the fact that the Holy Spirit liberates human persons *from* those experiences that oppress in mind, body, and spirit and *for* a radical sense of mission that carries forward into the reign of God.

Despite the myriad of references in the New Testament to the Holy Spirit as a distinct, active, and personal Being, however, there was no shortage of theological challenges to the Personhood of the Holy Spirit in the first centuries of Christendom. While most controversies involved the Trinity as a whole, two specifically concerned the Person and divinity of the Holy Spirit: Macedonianism, also known as Pneumatomachianism, and the filioque debate. Chapter Two discusses the main areas of dispute within these challenges and presents patristic, creedal, and contemporary responses to these controversies.

Since little is said in fact about the Holy Spirit in the Creeds in comparison to what is proclaimed about the First and Second Persons of the Trinity, one must delve not only into the Biblical witness, but also into the developing Christian tradition, to glean what distinguishes the Personhood of the Holy Spirit. Chapter Three presents "nascent pneumatologies" addressing the personal distinctiveness of the Holy Spirit. Theologians in this chapter offer substantial insights into the Personhood and agency of the Holy Spirit within both the Trinity and the believer that would influence centuries of thought to come. Among the most prominent in this chapter are Basil the Great from the East and Augustine of Hippo from the West.

Chapters Four and Five move from the influential insights of the patristics to contemporary pneumatologies which, by and large, approach the subject from a classical hermeneutic—that is, an interpretative perspective that makes universal claims concerning the Holy Spirit and presumes them to be applicable to every person in every time and place without distinction. Some of these pneumatologies reflect their specific religious tradition as a whole, while others reflect particular trajectories within a broader tradition. These selections are not meant to be exhaustive. Nonetheless, they do provide a representative sampling of the rich fare available in the Christian tradition concerning the liberating action of the Holy Spirit in human life. The offerings begin in Chapter Four with pneumatologies from Pentecostal and Protestant traditions, focusing on the work of Evangelical theologian Ben Engelbrecht and Reformed theologian Jürgen Moltmann and conclude in Chapter Five with Eastern Orthodox and Roman Catholic pneumatologies, including those of Karl Rahner on the experience of the Spirit as grace, Hans Urs von Balthasar on the Spirit as the ecstatic love of God, and Yves Congar on pneumatological anthropology.

Chapter Six makes the turn from classical perspectives to specifically contextual approaches to pneumatology. The contextual approach began to appear in the 1960s and presented a distinctly different approach to doing theology, one explicitly "bound to," and shaped by, "a particular historical, socio-cultural, political, and psychological life-situation."[4] In this movement, pneumatology has come to be understood as "a dynamic, thoughtful activity that seeks to bring a religious tradition into genuine conversation with some aspect of contemporary experience."[5] Over time, interaction with the social, historical, and cultural particularities of a variety of theologians and their communities have yielded pneumatologies viewed through the human experiences of women, African-Americans, Latinos and Latinas, and persons who are poor and oppressed throughout the world. Chapter Six explores the irruption of the Holy Spirit in Latin American liberation pneumatology. In so doing, the text makes its theme of liberation all the more explicit through the writings of Gustavo Gutiérrez from his book *The God of Life*, José Comblin on the Holy Spirit from *Mysterium Liberationis*, and Leonardo Boff on the pneumatization of Mary from *Come, Holy Spirit: Inner Fire, Giver of Life & Comforter of the Poor*.

Chapter Seven turns to the Holy Spirit disclosed in feminist pneumatological discourse. Theologian Helen Bergin argues for the

---

4   Emmanuel Clapsis, "The Challenge of Contextual Theologies," *GOTR* 38 (1993): 73.

5   Brennan Hill, Paul Knitter, and William Madges, *Faith, Religion, Theology: A Contemporary Introduction* (Mystic, CT: Twenty-Third Publications, 2002), 287.

Silenced

significance of attention to the topic "because it brings together two voices often rendered silent in mainstream theology, namely the Spirit of God and women."[6] Bergin lays out five "initial concerns" that feminist theologians encounter in formulating a feminist pneumatology, and these are addressed in turn by Colombian theologian Patricia Urueña Barbosa, reflecting on the Biblical symbol of Spirit-Wisdom; womanist theologian Linda Thomas, presenting pneumatology as Black women's "memory of the future"; and feminist theologian Elizabeth Johnson, offering Spirit-Sophia as Divine Livingness.

Chapters Eight and Nine pivot to pneumatological insights specifically rooted in the context of the United States. As James Cone wrote concerning the Holy Spirit in the African-American context, "God's manifestation as Spirit is indispensable for a total picture of the Christian God…. The Holy Spirit is the power of God at work in the world effecting in the life of his people his intended purposes."[7] While there is a significant amount of writing on the Holy Spirit from the perspective of the Black church, Black spirituality, and eschatological liberation, there is, however, far less systematic pneumatological research on the liberative activity of the Holy Spirit in the Black community. Nonetheless, Chapter Eight offers cogent contributions from three Black theologians in this regard: James Cone, who reflects on the Holy Spirit and Black power; J. Deotis Roberts, who discusses the Holy Spirit and human liberation; and David Emmanuel Goatley, who presents his creative insight on the Holy Spirit as the improvisation of God.

Chapter Nine investigates pneumatologies that advance the hope of millions of Latinx persons in the United States experiencing xenophobia, along with its social, political, and economic disenfranchisement. Unfortunately, "one would be hard pressed to find any substantial work dealing explicitly with the work and nature of the Spirit in Latina/o theology."[8] Despite that challenge, the chapter presents three emerging Latinx pneumatologies. These focus on Néstor Medina, with

---

6   Helen Bergin, "Feminist Pneumatology," *Colloquium* 42:2 (2010): 188.

7   James Cone, *Black Theology and Black Power* (Maryknoll, NY: Orbis, 2018), 64.

8   Néstor Medina, "Theological Musings toward a Latina/o Pneumatology," in *The Wiley Blackwell Companion to Latino/a Theology*, ed. Orlando Espín, 174–89 (Malden, MA: John Wiley and Sons, 2015), 174.

his notion of *Convivencia*; Samuel Soliván, with his emphasis on the Personhood of the Holy Spirit; and Orlando Espín, with his proposal concerning a pneumatological hermeneutic for the apparition of Our Lady of Guadalupe.

In the final chapter, this text shifts from its dedicated focus on the Personhood of the Holy Spirit in human experience to explore the Spirit's manifestation in the broader cosmos to propose ways in which the Holy Spirit may be manifested through processes and structures present, active, and liberative in the universe. Employing concepts drawn from ecological science and modern physics, three manifestations of the Spirit in the cosmos are examined: "the Green Face of God" from Mark I. Wallace; Holy Spirit as field of force from Wolfhart Pannenberg; and my own proposal of Holy Spirit as the Strange Attractor in an evolving cosmos.

At the outset of this Introduction, I asked, "What might one expect of the Holy Spirit set free from prepositional limitation, unfettered by ecclesiological structures?" It is my sincere hope that the chapters that follow offer a viable response to that question, particularly from the perspective of liberation. While some may deem the omission of the explicitly spiritual, ecclesiological, and Christological a lacuna in this effort, I give the assurance that there is much in theological literature that would fill this perceived void. As the foundation for the present effort, I offer the insight of Leonardo Boff:

> To think of the Spirit is to think of movement, action, process, appearance, story, and the irruption of something new and surprising.... These are not things that can be described in classical concepts.... [We] need a different paradigm...[that] helps us see...the Unnamable, Mysterious, Loving Energy that...penetrates creation from beginning to end.[9]

May this book provide a step in that direction.

---

9   Leonardo Boff, *Come, Holy Spirit: Inner Fire, Giver of Life & Comforter of the Poor*, trans. Margaret Wilde (Maryknoll, NY: Orbis, 2015), viii.

CHAPTER ONE

The Person of the Holy Spirit

INTRODUCTION

FROM THE EARLIEST ATTEMPTS at articulating the Trinitarian nature of God, questions were raised about the Person of the Holy Spirit in the life of the Trinity.[1] Is the Holy Spirit the Spirit of God spoken of in the Hebrew Scriptures as the "mighty wind" who hovered over the waters of creation (Genesis 1:2), as the one poured out over all humankind as proclaimed in the book of Joel (3:1–2), and as the Spirit sent forth to renew the face of the earth (Psalms 104:30)? Is the Holy Spirit the Spirit of God in the Gospels who overshadowed Mary at her annunciation (Luke 1:35), who descended upon Jesus in the form of a dove at his baptism (Mark 1:10; Matthew 3:16; Luke 3:22), who drove Jesus into the desert after his baptism (Mark 1:12; Matthew 4:1; Luke 4:1), in whom Jesus prayed and rejoiced (Luke 10:21), who distributes spiritual gifts for the benefit of the community (1 Corinthians 12:4–11), and in whom we are sanctified (2 Thessalonians 2:13–14)? Or is the Holy Spirit the Spirit of Jesus whom Jesus breathed upon the disciples after the resurrection (John 20:21–23), who enables us to cry out, "Abba, Father" (Galatians 4:6), and who makes it possible for believers to belong to God (Romans 8:9)? Are these one and the same Holy Spirit? Is it the same Holy Spirit at work in creation, in incarnation, in grace, and in salvation?

---

1   Elements of this chapter appear in my book *Trinity in Relation: Creation, Incarnation, and Grace in an Evolving Cosmos* (Winona, MN: Anselm Academic, 2012).

The conclusion of those who posed the question was "yes." It is the same Holy Spirit who "can come mightily upon a human being (Judges 14:6; 1 Samuel 16:13) and 'clothe' that person for powerful works (Judges 6:34ff). The very same Spirit also enables humans to perform such deeds as the liberation of Israel by the judges (Judges 3:10, 6:34) or visions by the prophets (Ezekiel 3:12, 8:3, 11:1)."[2] The Holy Spirit who anoints charismatic leaders like Gideon (3:10), Jephthah (6:34), and Samson (13:25 and 14:6, 19) in the book of Judges is the Holy Spirit who anoints the Messiah in the books of the prophets. The prophet Isaiah speaks of the one who is "ordained and empowered by the Spirit" (11:1–8) and who accomplishes the salvation of the Jews and the Gentiles in the power of the Spirit (42:1–4, 49:1–6). The outpouring of God's Spirit brings about justice and peace (Isaiah 32:15–20), healing and restoration (Ezekiel 11:19ff., 18:31, 36:36ff.), and the new creation (Ezekiel 37:1–4). And it is the same Spirit who fills the prophet-Messiah Jesus of Nazareth (Luke 4:18–19) in whose ministry the reign of God breaks forth for the oppressed and afflicted. If it is the same Holy Spirit, however, what, if anything, distinguishes the Trinitarian Person of the Holy Spirit from the Spirit of the Divine who animated, vivified, and inspired the leaders and prophets of Israel? As theologian Gerald O'Collins puts it:

> What kind or amount of personal characteristics should lead to the conclusion that we face an ontologically distinct person? What indicates that we encounter not simply a new mode of divine action in salvation history but a distinct, personal presence?... [What] leads believers to move beyond Jewish ideas and recognize within God not only a distinct divine Son but also a distinct divine Spirit?[3]

While some, like O'Collins, point to the "conspicuously personal effects" that the Holy Spirit has in the ministry of Jesus of Nazareth,[4]

---

2   Veli-Matti Kärkkäinen, *Pneumatology: The Holy Spirit in Ecumenical, International, and Contextual Perspectives* (Grand Rapids, MI: Baker Academic, 2002), 27.

3   O'Collins, Gerald, *The Tripersonal God: Understanding and Interpreting the Trinity* (New York: Paulist Press, 2014), 166–67.

4   O'Collins, *The Tripersonal God*, 167.

such indications do not present compelling evidence of a unique personhood of the Holy Spirit as distinct from that of the Incarnate Son. The overshadowing of the Holy Spirit in the conception of Jesus (Luke 1:35), the impulse of the Spirit that drives Jesus into the desert (Mark 1:12; Matthew 4:1; Luke 4:1), the presence of the Spirit in the form of a dove at Jesus' baptism (Mark 1:10; Matthew 3:16; Luke 3:22) and in the form of a cloud at Jesus' transfiguration (Mark 9:1–8; Matthew 17:1–6; Luke 9:28–36), and the prohibitions about sins against the Holy Spirit (Mark 3:28–30; Matthew 12:30–32; Luke 12:8–10) lend clearer support for this uniqueness, especially when there is reference to or manifestation of the Father or Son as well.

Nonetheless, the question remains: How does any one of these provide evidence that fully differentiates the personhood of the Holy Spirit from the Incarnate Son who was sent? At what point does the Holy Spirit emerge in the Christian narratives in so novel a way as to constitute a unique and personal being and to necessitate a new way of speaking about the Holy Spirit?

THE PERSONHOOD OF THE HOLY SPIRIT

An indication of the distinct personhood and promise of the Holy Spirit is found in the words of Jesus himself in the Gospel of John. Here Jesus is clearly portrayed as the giver of the Spirit (cf. John 19:30 and 20:22).[5] Nonetheless, in the midst of the "farewell discourses" of Jesus in John 13–17, Jesus makes several references to the "Advocate" or "Paraclete" whom the Father will send. The term comes from the Greek word *parakletos*, which can be translated as "comforter," "counselor," "advocate, or "defender." Consider the five ways in which Jesus speaks about the Holy Spirit in the Gospel of John—four that use the term *Advocate* and one that implies such a role.

In John 14:16, Jesus tells his disciples: "I will ask the Father, and *he will give you another Advocate to be with you always, the Spirit of truth,* which the world cannot accept, because it neither sees nor knows it."

5 George T. Montague, "Fire in the Word: The Holy Spirit in Scripture," in *Advents of the Spirit: An Introduction to the Current Study of Pneumatology*, ed. Bradford E. Hinze and D. Lyle Dabney (Milwaukee: Marquette University Press, 2001), 49.

By referring to the Holy Spirit as "another" Advocate, Jesus clearly distinguishes the Holy Spirit from himself, even as he implies that he himself was the first advocate. In addition, Jesus differentiates the Spirit from the Father as well, since it is the Father who will send this new Advocate.

In John 14:26, Jesus elaborates: *"The Advocate, the Holy Spirit that the Father will send in my name will teach you everything and remind you of all that I told you."* Expanding the notion that he will ask the Father to send the Spirit of truth, Jesus further develops the character of the Spirit as a teacher in the Spirit's own right, even as he affirms that the Spirit reinforces what Jesus himself has taught.

In John 15:26, Jesus attributes the sending of the Holy Spirit not only to the Father, but also to the Son: *"When the Advocate comes whom I will send you from the Father, the Spirit of truth that proceeds from the Father,* he will testify to me." This corresponds to the relational distinction of persons through the dynamic within the Trinity of the Trinitarian processions. As Christians profess in the Nicene Creed, the Holy Spirit is the one "who proceeds from the Father and the Son." Moreover, the Spirit is now spoken of as a witness, one who testifies to what the Spirit has seen or heard, which further emphasizes the Personhood of the Spirit as distinct from the Father and the Son.

In John 16:7, Jesus definitively testifies to this distinction between the Spirit and himself: "I tell you the truth, it is better for you that I go. *For if I do not go, the Advocate will not come to you.* But if I go, I will send him to you." Two further insights about the Spirit emerge in this part of the discourse. On the one hand, the statement contends that the Son and the Spirit are mutually exclusive. According to Jesus, if he, the Son, remains, the Spirit does not come. On the other hand, the sending of the Spirit is now exclusively attributed to the Son rather than to the Father or the Father and the Son together.

Finally, in John 20:21–23, Jesus sends the Spirit in a different way: "Jesus breathed on [his disciples] and said to them, 'Receive the Holy *Spirit. Whose sins you forgive are forgiven them, and whose sins you retain are retained.'"* This clearly indicates a mission of the Spirit from Jesus himself and further develops the character and work of the Holy Spirit. In this context, the Spirit serves to counsel the disciples in discerning the forgiveness of sins.

This series of Jesus' sayings concerning the Holy Spirit promises something truly novel that amplifies the way of viewing and speaking about the Holy Spirit found in the Synoptics, particularly in Luke. From this novelty emerges a new sense of the Holy Spirit both in relation to the Father and the Son and in relation to the nascent Christian community.

THE PRESENCE AND POWER OF THE HOLY SPIRIT IN THE SYNOPTICS

In the Synoptic Gospels, there is further evidence of the distinct character of the Holy Spirit, if not in all cases the actual Personhood. This evidence is found, by all accounts, most clearly in the Gospel of Luke and, as will be seen later in this chapter, in its companion work, the Acts of the Apostles. The Gospel of Luke mentions the Holy Spirit more than a dozen times in the first four chapters of his Gospel. In comparison, Mark makes reference to the Holy Spirit six times and Matthew, seven times. As noted above, "Matthew and Mark, as well as Luke, refer to the Spirit in their accounts of the ministry of John the Baptist, the baptism of Jesus and his going into the wilderness to be tempted, although only Luke uses the phrase 'Holy Spirit' in relation to the last two incidents."[6] However, of particular note is the emphasis on the Holy Spirit found in the conceptions and births of John the Baptist and Jesus in the Gospel of Luke.

According to George Montague in his essay "Fire in the Word," the Holy Spirit in both the Gospel of Luke and Acts is the spirit of prophecy.[7] The Gospel of Luke introduces this activity of the Holy Spirit in the angel's prophecy to Zechariah about the conception of John, who himself will be "filled with the Holy Spirit even from his mother's womb" (1:15). John's ministry was to be that of prophet "in the spirit and power of Elijah" (1:17) to prepare Israel for the Lord. The Holy Spirit next overshadows Mary in the Annunciation (1:35), as it is through the Holy

---

6   Tony Benson, "The Holy Spirit in Luke's Gospel," *The Testimony* 73 (2007): 276–79.

7   Montague, "Fire in the Word," 49.

Spirit that she will conceive and bear a Son. Her kinswoman Elizabeth, too, is filled with the Holy Spirit (1:41) and prophesies that Mary is to be the mother of the Lord. Finally, when John is born to Elizabeth, it is the Holy Spirit who impels Zechariah to prophesy the salvation of Israel through the forgiveness of sins, a salvation prepared by the prophetic ministry of his son John (1:67).

The presence and power of the Holy Spirit continues to be manifest in the Gospel of Luke when Jesus is presented in the temple (2:25–27). There is found the righteous and devout Simeon "looking for the consolation of Israel, and the Holy Spirit was upon him." According to the narrative, the Holy Spirit had revealed to Simeon "that he should not see death before he had seen the Lord's Christ. Inspired by the Spirit he came into the temple" (2:26), took Jesus in his arms, and prophesied concerning Jesus in this way:

> Behold, this child is set for the fall and rising of many in Israel,
> and for a sign that is spoken against
> (and a sword will pierce through your own soul also),
> that thoughts out of many hearts may be revealed. (2:34–35)

Later in the Gospel of Luke, when John enacted his ministry of baptism in the region of the Jordan, his preaching of repentance and forgiveness of sins prompted his listeners to wonder if he were the Christ, the promised messiah. In his denial, John associates the ministry of Jesus the Christ with a new baptism, one not of water but "with the Holy Spirit and with fire" (3:16) that Montague associates with Jesus' ministry of preaching, healing, and exorcism.[8] John's proclamation concerning Jesus is ratified in Jesus' own baptism, when "the Holy Spirit descended upon him in bodily form, as a dove, and a voice came from heaven, 'You are my beloved Son; with you I am well pleased'" (3:22).

In his essay, Montague suggests several interpretations of the dove in this narrative. The first recalls the dove that returns after the great flood to Noah, signaling a new creation that is now initiated in the baptism of Jesus. The theme of creation also appears in the interpretation of the dove as the Spirit of God that hovered over the waters of creation. This association with the original creation signals the new

---

8   Montague, "Fire in the Word," 48.

creation emerging from Jesus' life and ministry.[9] Despite these positive connotations, the association of the Holy Spirit with the dove has led to an impersonal representation of the Holy Spirit, leading to many an artistic representation of the Trinity as "two men and a bird." This has had disastrous consequences theologically for the recognition of the full personhood, dignity, equality, and activity of the Holy Spirit in Christian tradition, life, and prayer. As Montague notes, "the dove image has enhanced the picture of the Holy Spirit [from the realm of physical nature] but not sufficiently to demand that the Holy Spirit be a separate hypostasis, a person."[10] It played no small part in conceiving the Holy Spirit "as a power [which] appeared graphically only in the form of the dove and thus receded, to a large extent, in the Trinitarian speculation."[11]

Nonetheless, the power of the Holy Spirit who descended upon him at his baptism became manifest in Jesus when he returned from the Jordan "full of the Holy Spirit." This Holy Spirit then led him into the wilderness for forty days (4:1), where he wrestled with temptation in the desert (4:2–13) to use the Spirit for his own ends.[12] Having survived this ordeal, Jesus returned to Galilee "in the power of the Spirit" and came on the Sabbath to teach in the synagogue. It is here, quoting from the book of the prophet Isaiah, that Jesus himself gives testimony to the presence and power of the Holy Spirit in his own life, which defines his mission and ministry.

> The Spirit of the Lord is upon me,
> because he has anointed me
> to preach good news to the poor.
> He has sent me to proclaim release to the captives
> and recovering of sight to the blind,

---

9   Montague, "Fire in the Word," 42.

10 Montague, "Fire in the Word," 42. Like this author, Montague notes that this occurs when Jesus refers to the Spirit as the Paraclete or Advocate in the Gospel of John.

11 "Christianity: The Holy Trinity," *Encyclopedia Britannica Online*, https://www.britannica.com/topic/Christianity/The-Holy-Trinity.

12 Benson, "The Holy Spirit," 278.

to set at liberty those who are oppressed,
to proclaim the acceptable year of the Lord. (4:18–19)

Clearly, Jesus' understanding of the power of the Holy Spirit was that of liberation—liberation from poverty, from captivity, from blindness and ignorance, and from oppression in order that a year acceptable to the Lord may emerge. This understanding of the presence and power of the Holy Spirit became the core of Jesus' own mission and ministry, a mission and ministry communicated in word and deed in his proclamation of the reign of God. His was a liberating pneumatology that shaped and directed his entire life's work.

THE HOLY SPIRIT IN ACTS AND THE EPISTLES

The Acts of the Apostles

Commonly considered a companion volume to the Gospel of Luke and attributed to the same author, the Acts of the Apostles has more than fifty references to the Holy Spirit. It opens with a promise from Jesus himself, who "charged [the disciples] not to depart from Jerusalem, but to wait for the promise of the Father, which, he said, 'you heard from me, for John baptized with water, but before many days you shall be baptized with the Holy Spirit'" (Acts 1:4–5). With this promise comes a mission.

In Acts 1:8, before his ascension, Jesus says to his disciples, "You will receive power when the Holy Spirit comes upon you, and you will be my witnesses in Jerusalem, throughout Judea and Samaria, and to the ends of the earth." This description attributes a further power to the Holy Spirit, one that enables disciples to bear witness to the words and deeds of Jesus, even as the Spirit witnesses to Christ. The fulfillment of this promise comes in the second chapter of Acts, in the narrative of Pentecost:

When the time for Pentecost was fulfilled, they were all in one place together. And suddenly there came from the sky a noise like a strong driving wind, and it filled the entire house in which they were. Then there appeared to them tongues as of fire, which parted and came to rest on each

one of them. And they were all filled with the Holy Spirit and began to speak
in different tongues, as the Spirit enabled them to proclaim. (Acts 2:1–4)

This is a narrative full of symbolic language: the rushing wind signals
a new and unexpected act of God within history (John 3:8); the tongues
of fire call to mind the fire of the presence of God in the giving of the
covenant on Sinai (Exodus 19:18). With fire, the Christian community
now must bear witness to a new covenant in the power of the Spirit,
one that reaches to all parts of the world, symbolized by the utterance
in different tongues. How did this power of the Spirit manifest itself
through the disciples? It enabled them to speak of the mighty deeds
of God in language that each one could understand despite the fact
that they were Jews from many disparate regions around Jerusalem
(2:6–11). It empowered them to testify fearlessly to the wonders and
signs that God had worked through Jesus (2:22), to proclaim his resurrection from the dead (2:32), and to call for repentance that those
who listened might have their sins forgiven and receive the Holy
Spirit (2:38).

From this momentous outpouring of the Spirit on the disciples at
Pentecost flow the activities of the Spirit in the early Christian community. In addition to the event of Pentecost, there are other significant
instances of the outpouring of the Holy Spirit on believers. According
to Luke Timothy Johnson, the Holy Spirit is the "life principle" of the
early Church.[13]

The Holy Spirit figures prominently in Acts 4, in which Peter and
John are arrested for preaching about Jesus' resurrection from the
dead and for healing in his name. When they were brought before the
religious authorities, they were asked by what power and by what name
they preached in this way.

Then Peter, filled with the Holy Spirit, said to them, "Rulers of the people and elders, if we are questioned today because of a good deed done to
someone who was sick and are asked how this man has been healed, let it be
known to all of you, and to all the people of Israel, that this man is standing
before you in good health by the name of Jesus Christ of Nazareth, whom

---

13 Luke Timothy Johnson, *The Acts of the Apostles* (Wilmington, DE: Michael
    Glazier, 1992), 14–18.

you crucified, whom God raised from the dead. (Acts 4:8–10)

Amazed by the boldness with which Peter and John spoke and "finding no way to punish them because of the people" (4:21), the religious leaders released Peter and John. When they returned to their friends to report what had happened, they all gathered in prayer and praise of God for the signs and wonders worked through Jesus. "When they had prayed, the place in which they were gathered together was shaken; and they were all filled with the Holy Spirit and spoke the word of God with boldness" (4:31).

Another event of significance in the early Church occurred during the visit of Peter to Cornelius, who was a Gentile (Acts 10). Sought out by Cornelius, who "was directed by a holy angel to send for [Peter] to come to his house and to hear what you have to say," Peter traveled to Caesarea to meet Cornelius, who had gathered his relatives and friends. When Peter asked why he had sent for him, Cornelius replied:

> Four days ago at this very hour, at three o'clock, I was praying in my house when suddenly a man in dazzling clothes stood before me. He said, "Cornelius, your prayer has been heard and your alms have been remembered before God. Send therefore to Joppa and ask for Simon, who is called Peter; he is staying in the home of Simon, a tanner, by the sea." Therefore I sent for you immediately, and you have been kind enough to come. So now all of us are here in the presence of God to listen to all that the Lord has commanded you to say. (10:30–33)

Moved by the testimony of Cornelius, Peter answered, "I truly understand that God shows no partiality, but in every nation anyone who fears him and does what is right is acceptable to him" (10:34–35). While Peter was still speaking to the Gentiles gathered there about Jesus, "the Holy Spirit fell upon all who heard the word" (10:44). This astonished the circumcised believers "that the gift of the Holy Spirit had been poured out even on the Gentiles, for they heard them speaking in tongues and extolling God" (10:45–46). Clearly, the Holy Spirit showed no partiality and was not limited simply to those who had already been baptized into Christ. In fact, it was the presence of the Holy Spirit that earmarked those ready to be baptized.

The Holy Spirit in the Pauline Literature

In addition to the Acts of the Apostles, the Holy Spirit plays a key role in the Pauline literature. According to Montague, there was in the Pauline churches a "highly developed pneumatology grounded solidly in the resurrection."[14] Paul identifies the Holy Spirit with the love of God, affirming that "God's love has been poured into our hearts through the Holy Spirit that has been given to us" (Romans 5:5) and asserts that the message of the gospel comes not only in word "but also in power and in the Holy Spirit and with full conviction" (1 Thessalonians 1:5). Paul also speaks of the Thessalonians as imitators of Christ who have "received the word with joy inspired by the Holy Spirit, so that you became an example to all the believers" (1 Thessalonians 1:6) and identifies the source of the Spirit as "God, who gives his Holy Spirit to you" (1 Thessalonians 4:8). According to James Dunn, receiving the Spirit "like Christ" and the source of the Spirit as God shapes the Pauline understanding of the relationship of Christians with God.[15] Thus, Gerald O'Collins notes, the imitation of Christ for Paul involves a readiness to be shaped by the Holy Spirit.[16]

> Those who live according to the Spirit set their minds on the things of the Spirit.... [T]o set the mind on the Spirit is life and peace.... [You] are in the Spirit, since the Spirit of God dwells in you. Anyone who does not have the Spirit of Christ does not belong to him.... If the Spirit of him who raised Jesus from the dead dwells in you, he who raised Christ from the dead will give life to your mortal bodies also through his Spirit that dwells in you. (Romans 8: 5, 6, 9–11)

Not only does the Spirit shape the life of the Christian in the image of Christ as Paul asserts in Romans, but the Spirit also aids Christians in their spiritual weakness, keeping them attuned to the will of God.

---

14   Montague, "Fire in the Word," 47.

15   James D.G. Dunn, *Theology of Paul the Apostle* (Edinburgh: T & T Clark, 2003), 418–20.

16   Gerald O'Collins, *A Concise Dictionary of Theology* (Edinburgh: T & T Clark, 2003), 115.

> Likewise the Spirit helps us in our weakness; for we do not know how to pray as we ought, but that very Spirit intercedes with sighs too deep for words. And God, who searches the heart, knows what is the mind of the Spirit, because the Spirit intercedes for the saints according to the will of God. (Romans 8:26–27)

From this attunement to the will of God, the Holy Spirit bestows gifts upon the community "for the common good" (1 Corinthians 12:7).

> Now there are varieties of gifts, but the same Spirit.... To each is given the manifestation of the Spirit for the common good. To one is given through the Spirit the utterance of wisdom, and to another the utterance of knowledge according to the same Spirit, to another faith by the same Spirit, to another gifts of healing by the one Spirit, to another the working of miracles, to another prophecy, to another the discernment of spirits, to another various kinds of tongues, to another the interpretation of tongues. All these are activated by one and the same Spirit, who allots to each one individually just as the Spirit chooses. (1 Corinthians 12:4–11)

As each one opens him/herself to the Holy Spirit, the Christian can enjoy the Spirit's fruits, "love, joy, peace, patience, kindness, generosity, faithfulness, gentleness, and self-control" (Galatians 5:22–23).

THE HOLY SPIRIT IN CHRISTIAN LIFE

George Montague points out that, according to the Scriptures, the Holy Spirit bestows several ongoing effects on the Christian and the community. These include the relational, transformative, and charismatic/ministerial.

Relational

According to Montague, "the relational character of the Holy Spirit is particularly emphasized by Paul."[17] The Holy Spirit is the one who enables the believer to call on "Abba! Father!" (Galatians 4:6) in

---

17   Montague, "Fire in the Word," 54.

imitation of the Son and in an act of children of God and heirs with Christ (Romans 8:15–17). In addition, the Holy Spirit enables the Christian to confess Jesus as Lord (1 Corinthians 12:3). This confession implies that the Holy Spirit is not only relational, but also revelational, according to Montague, revealing the depths of God (1 Corinthians 2:9–16) and the mysteries of Jesus (Ephesians 1:17).[18] Moreover, it is the Spirit who is the source of *koinonia*, the bond of community among believers (Philippians 2:1 and 2 Corinthians 13:13).[19]

Transformative

The transformative effect of the Holy Spirit has a mystical element to it.[20] Montague references a particular passage in 2 Corinthians to exemplify this aspect of the Holy Spirit's work.

> Now the Lord is the Spirit, and where the Spirit of the Lord is, there is freedom. And all of us, with unveiled faces, seeing the glory of the Lord as though reflected in a mirror, are being transformed into the same image from one degree of glory to another; for this comes from the Lord, the Spirit. (2 Corinthians 3:17–18)

In this passage, Montague, following Joseph Fitzmyer,[21] points out that it is clearly the Holy Spirit that is involved in the process by which believers are transformed into the image of Christ. Montague suggests that this notion of transformation has resonances with Hellenistic mysticism in "the transformation of the initiate into the seen image of God."[22] This is not a restoration of the image of God in which human-

---

18   Montague, "Fire in the Word," 54.

19   Montague, "Fire in the Word," 54.

20   Montague, "Fire in the Word," 56.

21   Joseph A. Fitzmyer, "Glory Reflected on the Face of Christ (2 Cor 3:7–4:6) and a Palestinian Jewish Motif," *Theological Studies* 42 (1981): 630–44.

22   See J. Behm, *Theological Dictionary of the New Testament (IV)*, ed. Gerhard Kittel and Gerhard Friedrich, trans. Geoffrey W. Bromiley (Grand Rapids, MI: Eerdmans, 1967): 757–58.

ity was created (cf. Genesis 1:27); rather, the image is that of the Lord Jesus to which the Christian is conformed (Romans 8:29) and "the glory of the Lord" into which one is transformed.[23]

Charismatic/Ministerial

A "neglected aspect of western pneumatology,"[24] the gift of charisms through the Holy Spirit is core to multiple Scriptural texts. As noted above, the anointing of Jesus by the Holy Spirit in his baptism served not only as a proclamation of his divine sonship, but also as the empowerment for his ministry and his proclamation of the reign of God. Moreover, 1 Corinthians makes it clear that the diversity of gifts for ministry, given to the members of the Christian community, has its source in one and the same Spirit (12:4–11). In the context of these gifts of the Holy Spirit for the common good, the Epistles sometimes speak of "grace," as in Ephesians 4:7, "But each of us was given grace according to the measure of Christ's gift," and in 1 Peter 4:10, "Like good stewards of the manifold grace of God, serve one another with whatever gift each of you has received." This association of the Holy Spirit with the concept of grace will become more prominent with the formal development of pneumatology, especially in the theology of Karl Rahner.

A LOOK AHEAD

Many other insights into the Holy Spirit follow in the chapters to come, rooted in the fertile ground of the Christian Scriptures. As the previous Biblical passages illuminated the Spirit's personal uniqueness within the Trinity, the Spirit is revealed in specific relation to both the Trinitarian Persons and the Christian community. The Holy Spirit is (1) distinct from the Father and the Son, (2) sent from both the Father and the Son, (3) advocate and counselor to the disciples and the nascent Christian community, (4) teacher of "everything," even beyond the revelation given by Jesus himself, (5) active remembrance

---

23   Montague, "Fire in the Word," 56.

24   Montague, "Fire in the Word," 57.

of all that Jesus taught, (6) power of proclamation of the Risen Christ, and (7) impetus for the spread of the Gospel. Clearly, this Holy Spirit is no longer an impersonal force, indiscernible from the Father and the Son. Remaining fully united with the Father and the Son, the Holy Spirit yet emerges in novel ways as fully personal and unique through the activity of the Spirit in history.

In this uniqueness, the Scriptures recognize the Holy Spirit as the love of God poured into human hearts and the power through which believers speak the word of God with boldness. Active in the life of each Christian, the Holy Spirit shows no partiality, helps us in our weakness, and intercedes with sighs too deep for words. The Holy Spirit bestows a myriad of gifts for the common good and enables the believer to enjoy the fruits of love, joy, peace, patience, kindness, generosity, faithfulness, gentleness, and self-control.

Were one to name the themes that run throughout these references to the Holy Spirit, with Montague, one would recognize the themes of relation with the Father and the Son, as well as with the members of the community; of transformation into the image of Christ by the Holy Spirit; and of the bestowal of charisms for the common good. Nonetheless, underlying all of these themes is surely the theme of liberation—from sin, from fear, from weakness, from partiality, from jealousy, from doubt, from ignorance—even from death. The Holy Spirit liberates human persons *from* all those experiences that oppress in mind, body, and spirit, and liberates them *for* a radical sense of mission—through relation, through transformation, and through ministry—that carries liberation forward into the reign of God.

FOR REFLECTION

- What scriptural passages have influenced your experience of the Holy Spirit?
- What is your experience of the Person of the Holy Spirit?
- How have you experienced the Holy Spirit as relational, transformative, or charismatic in your life or in the life of your community of faith?

FOR FURTHER READING

Fitzmyer, Joseph A. "Glory Reflected on the Face of Christ (2 Cor 3:7–4:6) and a Palestinian Jewish Motif." *Theological Studies* 42 (1981): 630–44.

Kärkkäinen, Veli-Matti. *Pneumatology: The Holy Spirit in Ecumenical, International, and Contextual Perspectives.* Grand Rapids, MI: Baker Academic, 2002.

Montague, George T. "Fire in the Word: The Holy Spirit in Scripture." In *Advents of the Spirit: An Introduction to the Current Study of Pneumatology,* ed. Bradford E. Hinze and D. Lyle Dabney. Milwaukee: Marquette University Press, 2001.

CHAPTER TWO

Pneumatological Challenges

INTRODUCTION

DESPITE THE MYRIAD OF references in the New Testament to the Holy Spirit as a distinct, active, and personal Being, there was no shortage of theological challenges to the personhood of the Holy Spirit in the first centuries of Christendom. Most of these challenges involved the Trinity as a whole. The heresy of modalism claimed that the Father, Son, and Holy Spirit were not three persons, but rather simply three modes or manifestations of God's activity. Subordinationism contested the equality of the three Persons and maintained that one or more of the Persons of the Trinity is of lesser rank or dignity than another. Tritheism contended that the Father, Son, and Spirit were three Gods, rather than one God in three distinct Persons. Of those specifically concerning the Holy Spirit, two are of most significance: Macedonianism, also known as Pneumatomachianism, and the filioque controversy.

CHALLENGES TO THE DIVINITY AND PERSONHOOD OF THE HOLY SPIRIT

Macedonianism

Macedonianism, which was also called the *Pneumatomachian* heresy, is the name given to the beliefs of a fourth-century sect that denied

the full personhood and divinity of the Holy Spirit. Known also as the
Semi-Arians or the *Pneumatomachi* ("fighters against the Spirit"),
the members of this group were named after Macedonius, a moder-
ate Arian theologian who was twice Bishop of Constantinople. The
Arians viewed the Holy Spirit as the first creature of the Son, and as
subordinate to the Son as the Son to the Father. Whether Macedonius
himself rejected the divinity of the Holy Spirit or an early Christian
sect had recognized an affinity between their denial of the divinity of
the Spirit and his form of Arianism is unclear, since the writings of
the Macedonians have been lost. Nonetheless, one can ascertain their
principal teachings from the great fourth-century outcry in defense of
the full divinity of the Holy Spirit.

   Orthodox Church history credits Athanasius, Bishop of Alexandria,
as a principal defender of the divinity of the Holy Spirit. Writing in the
mid-fourth century, Athanasius' letter to Bishop Serapion was written
to offer advice to a fellow bishop on how to respond to those Christians
who were holding the Holy Spirit to be a creature. Distressed,
Athanasius puts forth the basic error in belief:

> You write, beloved and truly longed for, yourself also in distress, that cer-
> tain persons, having forsaken the Arians on account of their blasphemy
> against the Son of God, yet oppose the Holy Spirit, saying that He is not only
> a creature, but actually one of the ministering spirits, and differs from the
> angels only in degree.[1]

Athanasius first resorts to the Old and New Testaments, especially the
Gospels and Epistles, and considers the Holy Spirit in the context of
the Trinity itself. The Spirit is the means by which believers drink from
the fountain of the Father, the Enlightener of all from the Radiance of
the Son, the One who makes believers children of God and members
of Christ.[2] Nonetheless, he clearly argues that nowhere in Scripture is

---

1   Athanasius, *The Letters of Saint Athanasius Concerning the Holy Spirit to Bishop
     Serapion*, trans. C.R.B. Shapland (London: Epworth Press, 1951), 30, para. 1.
     http://thegroveisonfire.com/books/Athanasius/Athanasius-Letters-to-Serapion-
     CRB-Shapland.pdf.

2   Athanasius, *The Letters of Saint Athanasius*, 42, para. 19.

the Holy Spirit referred to as an angel.

> Tell us, then, is there any passage in the divine Scripture where the Holy
> Spirit is found simply referred to as "spirit" without the addition of "of
> God", or "of the Father", or "my", or "of Christ" himself, and "of the Son",
> or "from me" (that is, from God), or with the article so that he is called not
> simply "spirit" but "the Spirit", or the very term "Holy Spirit" or "Paraclete"
> or "of Truth" (that is, of the Son who says, "I am the Truth"),—that, just
> because you heard the word "spirit", you take it to be the Holy Spirit?[3]

Basil of Caesaraea, with his Cappadocian counterparts Gregory of
Nazianzus and Gregory of Nyssa, is known for leading the battle against
this heresy and its adherents, as well as perfecting the Trinitarian theology of Athanasius.[4] In his treatise *On the Holy Spirit*, Basil proceeds
"to attack our opponents" who disputed the equality of the Holy Spirit
with the Father and the Son "on account of the difference of His nature
and the inferiority of His dignity."[5] To refute this error, Basil emphasized the words of Jesus in Matthew 28:19, "Go therefore and make
disciples of all nations, baptizing them in the name of the Father and
of the Son and of the Holy Spirit." He charged his detractors "to keep
the Spirit undivided from the Father and the Son, preserving, both in
the confession of faith and in the doxology, the doctrine taught them
at their baptism."[6]

> For he who does not believe in the Spirit does not believe in the Son, and
> he who has not believed in the Son does not believe in the Father...for it is

---

3   Athanasius, *The Letters of Saint Athanasius*, 31, para. 4.

4   "Fourth Century: New Heresies," *The Orthodox Faith, Vol. III, Church History*, https://
     oca.org/orthodoxy/the-orthodox-faith/church-history/fourth-century/
     new-heresies.

5   Basil of Caesaraea, *On the Holy Spirit*, Chapter X, in *Post-Nicene Fathers of the
     Christian Church*, Series II, vol. 8, ed. P. Schaff and H. Wace, *Myriobiblios*, http://
     www.myriobiblos.gr/texts/english/basil_spiritu_10.html.

6   Basil, *On the Holy Spirit*, Chapter X. Tertullian makes a similar reference in his
     treatise *Adversus Praxean* (*Against Praxeas*), §26, http://www.tertullian.org/arti-
     cles/evans_praxeas_eng.htm.

impossible to worship the Son, save by the Holy Ghost; impossible to call upon the Father, save by the Spirit of adoption.[7]

In addition to Basil, his brother Gregory of Nyssa[8] also wrote a polemic against the Macedonians who "accuse us of profanity for entertaining lofty conceptions about the Holy Spirit."[9] In response to assertions that the Holy Spirit has no communion with the Father and the Son and is thus inferior to them, Gregory asserts unequivocally that the Holy Spirit is God.

> We...confess that the Holy Spirit is of the same rank as the Father and the Son, so that there is no difference between them in anything, to be thought or named, that devotion can ascribe to a Divine nature. We confess that, save His being contemplated as with peculiar attributes in regard of Person, the Holy Spirit is indeed from God, and of the Christ, according to Scripture, but that, while not to be confounded with the Father in being never originated, nor with the Son in being the Only-begotten, and while to be regarded separately in certain distinctive properties, He has in all else, as I have just said, an exact identity with them.[10]

Christianity in the West wrote in defense of the divinity of the Holy Spirit as well. In the fourth century, the writings of Augustine summarized the tendencies of much of the Western patristic tradition to maintain the Spirit's equality with the Father and the Son by pointing out the Spirit's proceeding specifically from the Father when the equality of the Spirit with the Father and the Son was in question. Augustine affirms that the Holy Spirit, "the Gift of God," is equal to the Father and the Son, since "we may believe God [the Father] not to

---

7   Basil, *On the Holy Spirit*, Chapter XI, http://www.myriobiblos.gr/texts/english/
     basil_spiritu_11.html.

8   With Gregory of Nazianzus, Basil the Great and Gregory of Nyssa are known as
     the Cappadocians. The three were staunch defenders of the orthodox doctrine
     of the Trinity.

9   Gregory of Nyssa, "Against the Followers of Macedonius," trans. W. Moore and
     H.A. Wilson, *Elpenor.org*, https://www.elpenor.org/nyssa/holy-spirit.asp.

10   Gregory of Nyssa, "Against the Followers of Macedonius."

give a gift inferior to Himself." Nonetheless, in Chapter IX of his work *De Fide et Symbolo* (On Faith and Creed),[11] Augustine admits his lack of clarity concerning the Person of the Holy Spirit, "since there has not been as yet, on the part of learned and distinguished investigators of the Scriptures, a discussion of the subject full enough or careful enough to make it possible for us to obtain an intelligent conception of what also constitutes His special individuality."[12] Despite the lack of a full investigation, Augustine concludes that Biblical scholars do hold that the Holy Spirit is not begotten *like* the Son, nor begotten *by* the Son, "like a Grandson of the Supreme Father." Rather, the Spirit "owe[s] that which he is...to the Father, of whom are all things."[13]

Filioque

Theological interest and interpretation concerning the distinction and unity of the Persons of the Trinity emerged within the first four centuries in both the East and West. Theologian Elizabeth Johnson relates a vignette attributed to fourth-century Eastern theologian Gregory of Nyssa concerning the widespread interest in these issues. As Johnson tells it,

> In the late fourth century...contemporaries, high and low, seriously engaged the question of how to speak about God. Their issue, in a culture awash with Greek philosophical notions, was whether Jesus Christ was truly divine or simply a creature subordinate to God the Father. The question engaged not only theologians or bishops but just about everybody. "Even the baker," wrote Gregory, "does not cease from discussing this, for if you ask the price of bread, he will tell you that the Father is greater and the Son subject to him."[14]

---

11 Augustine, *A Treatise on Faith and the Creed [De Fide et Symbolo]*, trans. S.D.F. Salmond, *EWTN*, https://www.ewtn.com/catholicism/library/on-faith-and-the-creed-11741, 9.19, emphasis added.

12 Augustine, *A Treatise on Faith and the Creed*, 9.19.

13 Augustine, *A Treatise on Faith and the Creed*, 9.19.

14 Elizabeth A. Johnson, "A Theological Case for God-she: Expanding the Treasury of Metaphor," *Commonweal* (January 29, 1993): 9. Internal quote from Gregory of

Trinitarian Interpretation in the East

The interpretation of how diversity and unity coexist in the Trinity is based in Scripture as well as philosophy. Greek theologians such as the Cappadocians Basil the Great, Gregory of Nyssa, and Gregory of Nazianzus began with the Scriptures, specifically with Jesus' revelation of God as three Persons in the Gospels. They then set about to reason "How can the Three be One?" For the Cappadocians, the Three in this case—Father, Son, and Holy Spirit—were assured through revelation. What was not evident, however, was how these three shared the divine essence and were One God. To answer this question, Eastern theology turned to the notion of relation.

For the East, divine essence and trinitarian relation began with the Father and proceeded from the Father to the Son and Holy Spirit. Greek theology applied the term *Theos,* or God, principally to the person of the Father, rather than to a divine essence. As a result, Greek theologians saw the Father as the source and origin of the divine Persons in essence and relation to one another. The Son eternally proceeded from the Father as begotten, and the Holy Spirit eternally proceeded from the Father *through* the Son as the "breath of the Son."

For the Cappadocians, two particular concepts explained how the three divine persons could be conceived as equal to one another and as one God. The first was a form of relation captured by the concept of *perichoresis.* This term comes from the Greek words *peri* and *choreio,* meaning "to move around" or "to dance around." Theologically, it was used to refer to the dynamic interpermeation of the three Persons of the Trinity, one in another while yet retaining their unique Personhood. According to John of Damascus, *perichoresis* refers to "the peculiarity of the relations of the Three Divine Persons..., their Indwelling in each other, the fact that, while they are distinct they yet are in one another...which implies their equal and identical Godhead."[15]

Nyssa, *"De deitate Filii et Spiritu sancti,"* in *Patrologiae cursus completus, Series graeca,* in 161 volumes, ed. Jacques-Paul Migne (Turnholti, Belgium: Brepols, 1977), 46.557.

15 Philip Schaff, "Hilary of Poitiers, John of Damascus," n. 1569, in *A Select Library of the Nicene and Post-Nicene Fathers of the Christian Church,* http://www.ccel.org/ccel/schaff/ npnf209.txt.

The second relational concept is that of *recapitulation*. According to this doctrine, the Son and the Spirit proceed from the Father, are not separated from the Father, and are both contained in the Father. Hence, the Father is the source of their oneness with each other and, of course, with the Father as well. Together, the Son and Holy Spirit are the *dynameis*, or "dynamism," of the Father who as *Theos* extends divine existence to them. This union is so complete that, in the words of Gregory of Nazianzus, "No sooner do I conceive of the One than I am illumined by the splendor of the Three; no sooner do I distinguish them than I am carried back to the One.... When I contemplate the Three together, I see but one torch, and cannot divide or measure out the undivided light."[16]

Trinitarian Interpretation in the West

Western theology was equally "awash with Greek philosophical notions," particularly those of essence and relation. Rather than beginning with the revelation in the Gospels, theologians from Western theology began their inquiry into the mystery of Trinity through the traditional belief in monotheism. Because of this approach, Western thinkers began with a different question than their Eastern counterparts. For them, the question was "How can the One God be Three?" For the theologians of the West, monotheism, the Oneness of God, was assured by Scripture and tradition. However, they needed to determine how God who is One could be understood as having three distinct persons. To accomplish this, theologians turned to the categories of the Greek philosophical traditions.

Foundational among them was theologian and bishop Augustine of Hippo, whose thought was not only influenced by the beliefs and traditions of Christianity, but also by the philosophy of Plato. Plato taught that there was a single transcendent source of all being, which he termed the *One*. According to Plato, the One is the Source of Being and existence, but is nonetheless beyond all being and existence. Therefore, the "One" remains absolutely transcendent, and nothing can be said of it except

---

16   Quoted by F. Scott Petersen in "Perichoresis," *Ars Theologica: An Intersection of Theology, Poetry, Art, and Music,* http://arstheologica.blogspot.com/2005/12/perichoresis.html.

that it is "One." Because Christianity's vision of God was monotheistic, Augustine saw the similarity between this Platonic concept of the One and Christian monotheism. Nonetheless, Christianity also professed that this One Source of Being existed as three Divine Persons. Therefore, to speak about Trinity authentically within both a Platonic and Christian worldview, Augustine realized that he had to clearly demonstrate how the One could be Three and yet remain One. Like the Greek theologians, he turned to the concept of relation.

Nonetheless, the philosophical tradition presented a theoretical difficulty for him in trying to understand the inner life of the Trinity in terms of relation. In philosophy, *relation* was one of the ten accidents and, therefore, not intrinsic to one's essence. Accidents, moreover, were changeable, and Augustine's concept of God held that God is unchangeable. Augustine realized, however, that the only way to speak of Three Persons as One God was to demonstrate their integral relation to one another. Thus, he had to reinterpret the concept of relation as it applied to the Trinity. Rather than conceiving relation as accidental to the Being of the Trinity, Augustine reinterpreted relation as "subsistent within," as essential to, the Being of the Trinity. If their relations are "subsistent," the Persons of the Trinity do not *have* relations, but in fact *are* relations. Moreover, these relations do not simply *exist in* but are *identical to* the divine essence, that is, to God's own self. Augustine's reinterpretation set the tone for subsequent Western theology by demonstrating that what constitutes the Trinitarian persons *as* persons are the relations that they *are* to one another.

> The three divine persons are mutually distinct only in and through their *relations of origin*. The internal relation between [sic] the three persons form their sole distinguishing feature. We can and should, for instance… [hold] that whatever we say about the Father we can also say about the Son except that he is the Father.… Thus the (subsistent) relations account for what differentiates (and unites) the one trinitarian reality.[17]

Or, as the venerable theologian Thomas Aquinas would say centuries

---

17   Gerald O'Collins, *The Tripersonal God: Understanding and Interpreting the Trinity* (New York: Paulist Press, 1999), 178, emphasis added.

later, "Distinction in God arises only through relation."[18] Because of this, *person* equals *relation* equals *essence*, making the divine essence the basis of Trinitarian unity.

The Filioque Controversy

While the East and West were of one accord in defending the Personhood of the Holy Spirit as equal to and distinct from the Father and the Son, over time consensus did not exist regarding the relationship of the Holy Spirit within the Trinity. Trinitarian theology uses the word *procession* to discuss and define the relationships among the Persons within the Trinity. In both the East and the West, the fact that the Son *proceeds* directly from the Father was unequivocal. Nonetheless, the procession or relationship of the Holy Spirit to the Father and the Son did not enjoy the same unanimity. There is an irony in this, as noted by Walter Cardinal Kasper in his book *That All May Be One: The Call to Unity Today.* "According to the Holy Scriptures and in the tradition of the Church," Kasper writes, "the Holy Spirit is the spirit of unity, the bond of love." Nonetheless, he continues, "Ecumenically we find ourselves in a rather paradoxical situation. The Spirit unites, but East and West have been at odds over the doctrine of the Holy Spirit for a thousand years."[19] The source of this division is most often referred to as "the *filioque* controversy."

The term *filioque* is a Latin word that is translated "and the Son." It refers to the statement of belief found in the Nicene-Constantinopolitan Creed and proclaimed in the Roman Catholic liturgy that the Holy Spirit "proceeds from the Father *and* the Son."[20] In contrast, Eastern Orthodox Christianity asserts that the Holy Spirit "proceeds from the Father *through* the Son,"[21] as articulated, for example, by the third-century theologian Origen of Alexandria.

---

18 Aquinas, *ST*, Ia.29.4.

19 Walter Kasper, *That All May Be One: The Call to Unity Today* (New York: Bloomsbury, 2004), 96.

20 "The Nicene Creed," United States Conference of Catholic Bishops, http://www.usccb.org/beliefs-and-teachings/what-we-believe/.

21 "The Creed: The Symbol of Faith," Orthodox Church in America, https://www.oca.org/orthodoxy/prayers/symbol-of-faith.

We believe, however, that there are three persons: the Father and the Son and the Holy Spirit; and we believe none to be unbegotten except the Father. We admit, as more pious and true, that all things were produced through the Word, and *that the Holy Spirit is the most excellent and the first in order of all that was produced by the Father through Christ.*[22]

In his writings, Western theologian Tertullian also maintained that the Holy Spirit proceeded "from the Father through the Son."[23] Using his colorful metaphors for the relationship of Father-Son-Holy Spirit as root-shoot-fruit, spring-river-irrigation canal, and sun-beam-illumination, Tertullian set out the steps through which the Son and Holy Spirit proceeded from the Father in the Trinity. First, discussing the Son, Tertullian wrote:

For God brought forth the Word...as a root *brings forth* the ground shoot, and a spring the river, and the sun its beam.... You need not hesitate to say that the shoot is *son of the root* and the river *son of the spring* and the beam *son of the sun*, for every source is a parent and everything that is brought forth from a source is its offspring.[24]

When he moves to the Holy Spirit, Tertullian's metaphor clearly implies that the Holy Spirit flows forth from the Father "out of" the Son.

[As] the fruit *out of the shoot* is third from the root, and the irrigation canal *out of the river* third from the spring, and the illumination point *out of the beam* third from the sun: yet in no respect is he alienated from that origin from which he derives his proper attributes.[25]

While it is difficult to discern whether "out of the Son" meant "through the Son" or "and the Son," Tertullian seems to clarify his insight by

---

22   Origen, *Commentary on the Gospel of John*, Book II, http://www.newadvent.org/fathers/101502.htm, emphasis added.

23   Tertullian, *Adversus Praxean*, §4, "I reckon the Spirit from nowhere else than from the Father through the Son."

24   Tertullian, *Adversus Praxean*, §8, emphasis added.

25   Tertullian, *Adversus Praxean*, §8, emphasis added.

indicating that the Spirit is in "no respect...alienated from that *origin* [i.e., the Father] from which he derives his proper attributes." Nonetheless, such confusion in terminology persisted into the fourth century, as demonstrated in the writings of two influential fourth-century theologians: Augustine and Hilary of Poitiers.

Focusing upon the scriptures and the creeds, Augustine affirms the Father as the origin of the divinity of the Son, who shares "the same life as the Father, God from God, light from light."[26] Furthermore, Augustine distinguishes the origination of the Spirit from that of the Son by speaking of the *procession* of the Spirit in contrast to the *begottenness* or *generation* of the Son. While Augustine begins with an understanding of the Holy Spirit as proceeding from the Father, he ultimately moves to affirming the Holy Spirit's procession from the Father and the Son:

> Neither can we say that the Holy Spirit does not also proceed from the Son, for the same Spirit is not without reason said to be *the Spirit both of the Father and of the Son*. Nor do I see what else He intended to signify, when He breathed on the face of the disciples, and said, "Receive the Holy Ghost." For that bodily breathing, proceeding from the body...was not the substance of the Holy Spirit, but a declaration by a fitting sign, that the Holy Spirit *proceeds not only from the Father, but also from the Son*.[27]

Later, Augustine augments this statement when, like other patristic theologians of his time, he views the Holy Spirit as the "love common to both [the Father and the Son], namely, the Holy Spirit."[28]

Writing in the midst of the ongoing Arian heresy, Hilary of Poitiers also formulated his work on the Holy Spirit in the context of his Trinitarian theology. In the process, Hilary specifically professes the

---

26 Augustine, *De fides et symbolo*, 4.6 in *On Christian Belief*, ed. Boniface Ramsey (Brooklyn, NY: New City Press, 2005), 160.

27 Augustine, *On the Trinity*, 4.29, in *Nicene and Post-Nicene Fathers, First Series*, Vol. 3, ed. Philip Schaff (Buffalo, NY: Christian Literature Publishing Co., 1887); rev. and ed. for *New Advent* by Kevin Knight, http://www.newadvent.org/fathers/1301.htm, emphasis added.

28 Augustine, *On the Trinity*, 15.10, 12.

Holy Spirit as "proceeding...from Father *and* Son."[29] Moreover, commenting on John 16, Hilary writes:

> Accordingly, He [the Holy Spirit] receives from the Son, *Who is both sent*
> *by Him*, and *proceeds from the Father*. Now I ask whether to receive from the
> Son is the same thing as to proceed from the Father. But if one believes that
> there is a difference between receiving from the Son and proceeding from
> the Father, *surely to receive from the Son and to receive from the Father will be*
> *regarded as one and the same thing*.[30]

However, Hilary seems to equivocate on this teaching in his final section, which he conceived in the form of a prayer to the Father. He prays, "Your Holy Spirit...proceeds *from* You [the Father] and is sent *through* Him [the Son]"[31]; this truth "I hold fast in my consciousness... that Your Holy Spirit is *from* You and *through Him*, although I cannot by my intellect comprehend it."[32]

WHAT IS AT STAKE IN THE DISTINCTION?

What is the difference between *through* and *and*? Eastern Orthodox Metropolitan Kallistos Ware (Timothy Ware) explains its significance in his book *The Orthodox Church*. Procession of the Holy Spirit from the Father and the Son, according to Ware, "impairs the proper balance within Trinitarian theology between the three distinctive persons and the shared essence."

> What holds the Trinity together? The Cappadocians, followed by later
> Orthodox theologians, answer that there is one God because there is one
> Father. The other two persons trace their origin to the Father and are

---

29   Hilary of Poitiers, *On the Trinity*, 2.29, in E.W. Watson and L. Pullan, Nicene
      and Post-Nicene Fathers, Second Series, Vol. 9, ed. Philip Schaff and Henry
      Wace (Buffalo, NY: Christian Literature Publishing Co., 1899); rev. and ed. for
      New Advent by Kevin Knight, http://www.newadvent.org/fathers/330212.htm.

30   Hilary of Poitiers, *On the Trinity*, 8.20, emphasis added.

31   Hilary of Poitiers, *On the Trinity*, 13.55, emphasis added.

32   Hilary of Poitiers, *On the Trinity*, 13.56, emphasis added.

defined in terms of their relation to Him. As the sole source of being within the Trinity, the Father constitutes in this way the principle or ground of unity for the Godhead as a whole. But...the west, in regarding not only the Father but also the Son as the source of the Spirit, finds its principle of unity, no longer in the *person* of the Father, but in the *essence* which the three persons share.[33]

According to Orthodox theologian Vladimir Lossky, "The Greek Fathers always maintained that the principle of unity in the Trinity is the Person of the Father."[34] This makes the Father the sole source of divinity from which the Son and Spirit proceed. Thus, what is at stake in the theological disagreement between East and West on the matter of the Holy Spirit is the broader question of what unites the three Persons of the Trinity as one God. In other words, "How can the Three be One?" and, conversely, "How can the One be Three?" Despite their agreement on relation as the essence of Trinitarian unity, the filioque controversy revealed deeper theological differences in how relation is actually operative within the Triune life of God.

THE CREEDS

Despite the significance to both the East and the West of these theological distinctions on the procession of the Holy Spirit, the expansion of the controversy and the inclusion of *filioque* in the creed of the Roman Church are a matter of some uncertainty.[35] The Nicene Creed of 325 CE focused primarily on the heresy that denied the divinity of the Son. As a result, it merely gives passing mention to the Holy Spirit compared to the proclamations concerning the Son.

---

33   Timothy Ware, *The Orthodox Church: An Introduction to Eastern Christianity*, 2nd rev. ed. (London: Penguin, 1993), Kindle ed., 208, emphasis in original.

34   Vladimir Lossky, *The Mystical Theology of the Eastern Church* (Cambridge, UK: James Clarke and Co., Ltd., 1957), 58.

35   United States Catholic Conference of Bishops (USCCB), "The Filioque: A Church Dividing Issue?: An Agreed Statement," October 25, 2003, Washington, DC, http://www.usccb.org/beliefs-and-teachings/ecumenical-and-interreligious/ecumenical/orthodox/filioque-church-dividing-issue-english.cfm.

We believe in…one Lord, Jesus Christ, the Son of God,
begotten from the Father, only-begotten, that is, from the substance of
the Father,
God from God, light from light, true God from true God,
begotten not made, of one substance with the Father,
through Whom all things came into being, things in heaven and things on earth,
Who because of us men and because of our salvation came down,
and became incarnate and became man, and suffered,
and rose again on the third day, and ascended to the heavens,
and will come to judge the living and dead,
And in the Holy Spirit.[36]

Nonetheless, this did not quell challenges to the full divinity and humanity of the Son, as well as to the divinity of the Holy Spirit. As a result, the Council of Constantinople in 381 CE not only reaffirmed the creed of Nicaea but also expanded it to include a more extensive affirmation concerning the Holy Spirit:

I believe in the Holy Spirit, the Lord, the giver of life,
who proceeds from the Father and the Son,
who with the Father and the Son is adored and glorified,
who has spoken through the prophets.[37]

Eventually, the stimulus of patristic theologians like Hilary and Augustine influenced the addition of the *filioque* to the Creed of Constantinople, which, combined with the Creed of Nicaea, became the normative statement of faith in the West.

When, in 1014, "the Creed, including the *Filioque,* was sung for the first time at a papal Mass…the liturgical use of the Creed, with the *Filioque,* now was generally assumed in the Latin Church to have the sanction of the papacy." [38] This assumption provoked rancorous

------

36   "The Creed of Nicaea—Agreed at the Council in 325," *Early Church Texts*, https://
earlychurchtexts.com/public/creed_of_nicaea_325.htm.

37   "The Nicene Creed," United States Conference of Catholic Bishops, http://www.
usccb.org/beliefs-and-teachings/what-we-believe/.

38   USCCB, "The Filioque."

ecclesial and political disputes from both directions, including councils, depositions, accusations of infidelities, and excommunications. These clashes ultimately culminated in 1054 in a schism between Eastern and Western Christianity. While it is too facile to suggest that any single event in this series of controversies led to the formal schism between the West and the East, the affirmation of the *filioque* served to "deepen the growing estrangement between Constantinople and Rome."[39]

A LOOK AHEAD

While a good deal of the discussion of the Holy Spirit in the early church focused upon questions concerning the Trinity as a whole, it is obvious that interest in the Holy Spirit involved a good deal of contention. Within the Church as a whole, the questions became consuming and, to a great extent, divisive. Nonetheless, as theological reflection on the person of the Holy Spirit moved forward, theologians produced a number of understandings of the Spirit that were cogent, beautiful, and even consistent between the East and West. Primary among these theologians were Basil the Great in the East and Augustine of Hippo in the West, both of whom moved the conversation and the understanding of the Holy Spirit in Christian life in compelling ways.

FOR REFLECTION

- Have you experienced the Holy Spirit as personal, as Person? Reflect on that experience.
- What is your experience of the unity in the Trinity? What draws them together as One?
- How does the Spirit attract you into the life of the Trinity? Describe that sense of attraction.

---

39 USCCB, "The Filioque."

FOR FURTHER READING

Augustine of Hippo. *The Trinity (Works of Saint Augustine: A Translation for the 21st Century)*, ed. John E. Rotelle, OSA; trans. Edmund Hill, 2nd ed. Hyde Park, NY: New City Press, 2012.

Kasper, Walter. *That All May Be One: The Call to Unity Today.* New York: Bloomsbury, 2004.

O'Collins, Gerald. *The Tripersonal God: Understanding and Interpreting the Trinity.* New York: Paulist Press, 1999.

United States Catholic Conference of Bishops (USCCB). "The Filioque: A Church Dividing Issue? An Agreed Statement," October 25, 2003, Washington, DC, http://www.usccb.org/beliefs-and-teachings/ecumenical-and-interreligious/ecumenical/orthodox/filioque-church-dividing-issue-english.cfm.

CHAPTER THREE

Nascent Pneumatologies

INTRODUCTION

A S DEMONSTRATED IN THE last chapter, little is said about the Holy Spirit
in the Creeds in comparison to what is proclaimed about the First and
Second Persons of the Trinity. The Holy Spirit is acknowledged as "the
Lord and Giver of Life," a life-giving characteristic that the Holy Spirit
shares with the Father and the Son. The unique affirmation made of the
Holy Spirit in the creed is that the Holy Spirit has "spoken through the
prophets," an attribute shared with the Son as the Word of God spoken
in prophecy. One must therefore delve into the Biblical witness and the
Christian tradition to glean what distinguishes the Holy Spirit. Many think
that the most obvious distinction lies in the presumption that the Holy
Spirit is non-personal. This thinking played no small part in conceiving
the Holy Spirit as a power that appeared only in the form of the dove, which
depreciated its place in Trinitarian speculation. However, two early theologians from the East and the West offered substantial insights into the
personhood and agency of the Holy Spirit within the Trinity and Christian
life. These are Basil the Great and Augustine of Hippo, respectively.

THE HOLY SPIRIT FROM THE EAST AND THE WEST

Basil the Great

Basil the Great was one of the staunchest advocates of the divinity of
the Holy Spirit. As discussed above, he was one of the fourth-century

Cappadocian Fathers who contributed significantly to the development of Orthodox Trinitarian theology. He wrote his work *On the Holy Spirit* (c. 375) in the midst of the controversy over the term *homoousios* (of one essence), used in the Creed of Nicaea to describe the unity of the Father and the Son. Nonetheless, the controversy said little about the divinity of the Holy Spirit.

In his work *On the Holy Spirit*, Basil used several arguments to establish the Spirit's equality and divinity within the Trinity. Calling the Holy Spirit "Lord" demonstrated equal rank with the Father and the Son; the works of the Holy Spirit in illumination, sanctification and salvation, and creation signified divinity. However, it appears that Basil was hesitant to state directly that the *Holy Spirit was God*, since neither Scripture nor tradition made such an assertion. This omission notwithstanding, Basil's affirmation of the Holy Spirit's divinity is beyond doubt.[1] As one commentator writes, Basil was "One of the pioneers and strongest advocates of the divinity of the Holy Spirit in the age of the Church Fathers."

> A man of deep prayer and theological insight, Basil was granted an understanding of the Person and working of the Holy Spirit, both within the mysterious and hidden life of the Trinity itself and also within the world of time and space, in the whole of creation as well as in the hearts and minds of individual believers.[2]

Basil wrote eloquently of the dwelling place of the Holy Spirit not only within the Trinity but also in "the world of time and space." Nonetheless, he is quite careful to distinguish these relationships.

> In relation to the originate [creation], then, the Spirit is said to be in them "in divers portions and in divers manners," while in relation to the Father

---

1   Saint Gregory Nazianzen, *Oration XLIII: Panegyric on Saint Basil*, ed. Philip Schaff and Henry Wace; trans. Charles Gordon Browne, M.A., and James Edward Swallow (Grand Rapids, MI: Eerdmans, 1983), Chs. 68–69.

2   The Community of the Holy Cross, "The Place of the Holy Spirit: Insights from the Teaching of St. Basil the Great," https://holycrosschc.org.uk/wp-content/uploads/2011/07/Holy-Spirit-St-Basil.pdf.

and the Son it is more consistent with true religion to assert Him not to be *in* but to be *with*. For the grace flowing from Him when He dwells in those that are worthy, and carries out His own operations, is well described as existing in those that are able to receive Him. On the other hand His essential existence before the ages, and His ceaseless abiding with Son and Father, cannot be contemplated without requiring titles expressive of eternal conjunction.[3]

Expressing the relationship between the Holy Spirit and creation, moreover, Basil is quite clear about his deliberate use of the preposition *in*.

It is an extraordinary statement, but it is nonetheless true, that the Spirit is frequently spoken of as the place of them that are being sanctified.... It follows that the Spirit is verily the place of the saints and the saint is the proper place for the Spirit, offering himself as he does for the indwelling of God.[4]

Thus, while the "saint" is *in* the Spirit, the Spirit is also *in* the "saint." Through the Spirit "we become intimate with God,"[5] which leads in Basil's mind to true worship. As Basil writes, "All things thirsting for holiness turn to Him; everything living in virtue never turns from Him."[6] Moreover, the Spirit liberates those in whom the Spirit dwells, frees them in their pursuit of holiness, and "helps them reach their proper fulfillment,"[7] especially in their service to others. Like Tertullian, his counterpart, Basil finds the image of the sunbeam useful in referring to the effect of the Holy Spirit on those imbued with the Spirit's presence.

---

3   Basil the Great, *On the Holy Spirit*, §63, *from Post-Nicene Fathers of the Christian Church*, Series II, ed. Henry Wace and Philip Schaff, http://www.myriobiblos. gr/texts/english/basil_spiritu_26.html, emphasis added.

4   Basil the Great, *On the Holy Spirit*, §62, emphasis added.

5   St. Basil the Great, *On the Holy Spirit*, trans. David Anderson (Crestwood, NY: St Vladimir's Seminary Press, 1980), §49.

6   Basil the Great, *On the Holy Spirit*, trans. Anderson, §22.

7   Basil the Great, *On the Holy Spirit*, trans. Anderson, §22.

Through [the Spirit's] aid hearts are lifted up, the weak are held by the hand, and they who are advancing are brought to perfection. Shining upon those that are cleansed from every spot, He makes them spiritual by fellowship with Himself. Just as when a sunbeam falls on bright and transparent bodies, they themselves become brilliant too, and shed forth a fresh brightness from themselves, so souls wherein the Spirit dwells, illuminated by the Spirit, themselves become spiritual, and send forth their grace to others.[8]

Those liberated by the power of the Holy Spirit "becomes like Moses, whose face shone with the glory of God's manifestation."

[As] objects placed near something brilliantly colored themselves become tinted through reflected light; likewise [the one] who fixes his gaze on the Spirit is transfigured to greater brightness…. Then the glory of the Holy Spirit is changed into such a person's own glory, not stingily, or dimly, but with the abundance we would expect to find within someone…enlightened by the Spirit.[9]

Augustine of Hippo

The most fruitful approach to exploring the pneumatology of Augustine of Hippo is through his treatise *On the Trinity* (*De Trinitate*). In his article "Gift and Communio: The Holy Spirit in Augustine's *De Trinitate*," Adam Kotsko claims that "for Augustine the Holy Spirit comes to be thought of as God in a privileged sense, that is, as the person of the Trinity who is the most proper bearer of certain privileged names of God, most notably love."[10] Thus, *On the Trinity* stands as a "particularly pregnant moment"[11] for Augustine's formulation of his pneumatology. Augustine viewed the Holy Spirit as gift and as love, particularly the love or communion shared between the Father and the Son.

---

8   Basil the Great, *On the Holy Spirit*, §23, Myriobiblos, http://www.myriobiblos. gr/texts/english/basil_spiritu_9.html.

9   Basil the Great, *On the Holy Spirit*, trans. Anderson, §52.

10   Adam Kotsko, "Gift and Communio: The Holy Spirit in Augustine's *De Trinitate*," *Scottish Journal of Theology* 64:1 (February 2011), 1.

11   Kotsko, "Gift and Communio," 1.

And if the love by which the Father loves the Son, and the Son loves the Father, ineffably demonstrates the communion of both, what is more suitable than that He should be specially called love, who is the Spirit common to both?... And yet it is not to no purpose that He is specially called the Holy Spirit; for because He is common to both, He is specially called that which both are in common.[12]

As a result, his pneumatology "determines his conception of the unity of God, the relationship of God to creation and, most importantly, what it means for God to be love."[13]

THE HOLY SPIRIT AS GIFT

The basis for Augustine's understanding of the Holy Spirit as *gift* comes from his efforts to distinguish between the procession of the Holy Spirit and of the Son from the Father. Augustine states that "[The Spirit] comes forth, you see, not as being born but as being *given*."[14] Echoing the insight of Basil, Augustine asserts, "So the Holy Spirit is not only the Spirit of the Father and of the Son who *gave* Him, but He is also called ours, who have received Him.... Therefore, the Spirit is both the Spirit of God who gave Him, and ours who have received Him."[15] The giftedness of the Holy Spirit is the Spirit's very nature from all eternity, for one can only be a gift if one is capable of being given. Thus, the Spirit is eternally "gift even before there was one to whom He might be given."[16] This makes the Holy Spirit uniquely both eternal and temporal, "a gift eternally, but a thing that has been given in time."[17]

In Augustine's further reflections on the Spirit as gift, "the Holy Spirit comes to be regarded as God in a privileged sense."[18] While

---

12   Augustine, *On the Trinity*, 15.37.

13   Kotsko, "Gift and Communion," 2.

14   Augustine, *On the Trinity*, 5.15, emphasis added.

15   Augustine, *On the Trinity*, 5.15.

16   Augustine, *On the Trinity*, 5.16.

17   Augustine, *On the Trinity*, 5.17.

18   Kotsko, "Gift and Communio," 5.

asserting that the name "Father" or "Son" could not be applied to the Trinity as a whole (5.12), he does maintain that the name "Holy Spirit" could be so applied.

> [Because] both the Father is a spirit and the Son is a spirit, and the Father is holy and the Son is holy. Therefore, since the Father, the Son and the Holy Spirit are one God, and certainly God is holy, and God is a spirit, the Trinity can be called also the Holy Spirit.[19]

Augustine understands this may not be wholly apparent in the names "Father" and "Son." He clarifies his understanding in reference once again to the Holy Spirit as gift, since, according to Scripture, the Holy Spirit "is the gift of the Father and of the Son."

> When we say, therefore, the gift of the giver, and the giver of the gift, we speak in both cases...[of] the Holy Spirit.... For He Himself is called specially that which they are called in common.... Therefore, that the communion of both may be signified from a name which is suitable to both, the Holy Spirit is called the gift of both.[20]

By setting forth this formulation, Augustine seems to locate the unity of the Trinity not in the monarchy of the Father, as in the East, nor in the divine nature shared, as in the West, but in the Holy Spirit, "which they are called in common," which is "the communion of both," and which is "the gift of both." Theologian Joseph Ratzinger, prior to becoming Pope Benedict XVI, drew this very conclusion:

> The particularity of the Holy Spirit is evidently that he is what the Father and Son have in common. His particularity is being unity...mutuality itself.... The mediation of Father and Son comes to full unity not...from a universally metaphysical substance but from the person.... The Spirit is Person as unity, unity as Person.[21]

---

19   Augustine, *On the Trinity*, 5.12.

20   Augustine, *On the Trinity*, 5.12.

21   Joseph Ratzinger, "The Holy Spirit as *Communio*: Concerning the Relationship of Pneumatology and Spirituality in Augustine," *Communio* 25 (Summer 1998): 326.

As a result, *communio* must be understood as "an essential element of the notion of the Spirit, thus truly giving it content and thoroughly personalizing it."[22] By understanding this, one can come to know who the Holy Spirit is and who God is. God as Spirit, Spirit as God, as *communio*, as mutuality, as gift, is love.

THE HOLY SPIRIT AS LOVE OR *COMMUNIO*

A second identification that Augustine gives the Holy Spirit is that of love or *communio*. "Whether we are to call Him that absolute love which joins together Father and Son, [or that which] joins us also from beneath,"[23] the Holy Spirit plays a critical role in Augustine's very conception of God "because love is bound up intimately with what it means to be God."[24]

Augustine develops this thought, beginning with the Scriptures 1 John 4:7–16 and Romans 5:5. The former gives him the meaning of love: "If we love one another, God abides in us and his love is perfected in us. By this we know that we abide in him and he in us, because he has given us of his own Spirit …. God is love, and he who abides in love abides in God, and God abides in him" (1 John 4:12, 13, 16).

A textual comparison yields the following insight for Augustine: "The Holy Spirit, of whom [God] has given us, causes us to abide in God, and God in us. But love does this. He is, therefore, the God who is love."[25] Augustine supports this insight through Romans 5:5: "God's love has been poured into our hearts through the Holy Spirit who has been given to us." This line of thought may be summarized thus: "The gift of God is the Holy Spirit. The gift of God is love. God communicates himself in the Holy Spirit as love."[26] For Augustine, therefore, the Holy Spirit is the one "through whom the two [Father and Son] are joined, through whom the Begotten is loved by the Begetter, and loves Him that begot Him."

---

22 Ratzinger, "The Holy Spirit as *Communio*," 327.

23 Augustine, *On the Trinity*, 7.6.

24 Kotsko, "Gift and Communio," 7.

25 Ratzinger, "The Holy Spirit as Communio," 328.

26 Ratzinger, "The Holy Spirit as Communio," 328.

Therefore the Holy Spirit, whatever it is, is something common both to the Father and Son. But that communion itself is consubstantial and co-eternal; and if it may fitly be called friendship, let it be so called; but it is more aptly called love.[27]

Coupling his understandings of the Holy Spirit as Gift and as Love, Augustine asserts:

There is no gift of God more excellent than [love].... Nor is the Spirit specially called the Gift, unless on account of love.... And therefore most rightly is the Holy Spirit, although He is God, called also the gift of God. And by that gift what else can properly be understood except love, which brings to God, and without which any other gift of God whatsoever does not bring to God?[28]

Moreover, since "the gift of the Holy Spirit is nothing else but the Holy Spirit" itself, the Holy Spirit is the Giver *and* the Gift and in both ways God.

Wherefore, if Holy Scripture proclaims that God is love, and that love is of God, and works this in us that we abide in God and He in us, and that hereby we know this, because He has given us of His Spirit, then the Spirit Himself is God, who is love.[29]

Citing Paul, Augustine insists that, while other gifts are also given by the Holy Spirit, "without love they profit nothing."[30] Clearly, to those to whom it is given, the gift that the Holy Spirit *gives* and the gift that the Holy Spirit *is*, is love.

These insights of Augustine on the Holy Spirit as love have woven throughout the theological tradition, even to the work of theologians today.[31] As explained in the words of Aquinas, for example,

---

27   Augustine, *De Trinitate*, 6.7.

28   Augustine, *De Trinitate*, 15.32.

29   Augustine, *De Trinitate*, 15.37.

30   Augustine, *De Trinitate*, 15.32.

31   Cf. Augustine, *On the Trinity*, 15.5.29–31; Aquinas, *Summa Theologiae* I:37.1;

> The Holy Spirit is called the bond between the Father and the Son, in that he is Love, since the Father loves the Son and the Son loves the Father by the one single love; thus the name of the Holy Spirit as Love implies a relation of the Father to the Son, that is to say a relation of the one who loves to the beloved one.[32]

Nonetheless, as Perfect Love, the Holy Spirit does not—in fact, can-not—reserve this love solely between the Lover and the Beloved. Thus was the claim of mystical theologian Richard St. Victor. To substantiate this claim, he developed the understanding of Love within the Trinity in a way that further distinguishes the uniqueness of the Holy Spirit.[33] Richard began with the model of Lover and Beloved as metaphors for the Father and the Son. However, Richard explicitly argued that love between two persons is less perfect than love shared among three "and that only when a third belongs to the circle of love is love perfected."[34] The Holy Spirit, therefore, is not solely the love between the Father and Son, but is the Third Person who completes the circle of love and thus assures the perfect love of the Trinity.

From the writings above emerges the understanding of the Holy Spirit as love *within* the Trinity. Nonetheless, as *communio* or *koino-nia*—variously translated as community, communion, participation, sharing and intimacy—the Spirit is also the impetus for relationships of love and creativity within history and between persons. As proclaimed by the theologian Hippolytus,

---

Summa Contra Gentiles IV: 20–22; Joseph Ratzinger, "The Holy Spirit as Communio: Concerning the Relationship of Pneumatology and Spirituality in Augustine," *Communio* 25 (1998): 324–37; Stanley Grenz, "The Holy Spirit: Divine Love Guiding Us Home," *Ex Auditu* 12 (1996): 1–13; Robert W. Jenson, *The Triune God* (New York: Oxford University Press, 1997), 146–61; Clark H. Pinnock, *Flame of Love: A Theology of the Holy Spirit* (Downers Grove, IL: InterVarsity Press, 1996), 37–40; David Coffey, "The Holy Spirit as the Mutual Love of the Father and the Son," *Theological Studies* 51 (1990): 193–229.

32   Aquinas, *Summa Theologiae* I:37.1.3.

33   Roger Olson and Christopher Alan Hall, *The Trinity* (Grand Rapids, MI: Eerdmans, 2002), 58–59.

34   Olson and Hall, *The Trinity,* 59.

> This is the Spirit that at the beginning moved upon the waters; by whom
> the world moves; by whom creation consists, and all things have life; who
> also wrought mightily in the prophets, and…was given to the apostles in
> the form of fiery tongues…. Of this Spirit Gabriel also spoke to the Virgin,
> "The Holy Ghost shall come upon you, and the power of the Highest shall
> overshadow you."[35]

Moreover, it is clear in both Augustine and in Richard St. Victor that
the Holy Spirit is "not simply an emotion or a sentiment," but rather
Love Personified.

Thus, love in its deepest sense is *personal* and *relational*; it is "the
divine Spirit who indwells us, awakens love within us, and draws us
into loving communion with God and others"[36] and who "fires [us]
to the love of God and neighbor."[37] As a result, the activity of the Holy
Spirit as gift, as love, as *communio*, is not merely a theological concept,
but has anthropological and cosmological consequences. Because of
this, those who seek to construct a liberative pneumatology must do so
through a renewed anthropology, "the anthropology of…human subjects whom the Spirit seeks to penetrate…by liberating, transforming, and reconciling, and who in turn are empowered to respond to
such overtures of the Spirit."[38] According to Anselm Min, the human
person is not primarily "an isolated soul, an individual subject…who
subsequently and accidentally enters into relations with others. It is
primarily…that of a being who finds itself 'always and already' existing
'in' the world."[39] Moreover, this world in which human persons exist
is a world that the Holy Spirit "creates and recreates…so as to unite all

---

35   Hippolytus, "The Discourse on the Holy Theophany," from *Ante-Nicene Fathers*,
     Vol. 5, ed. A. Roberts, J. Donaldson, and A.C. Coxe (Buffalo, NY: Christian
     Literature Publishing, 1886).

36   Patrick Franklin, "The God Who Sends Is the God Who Loves: *Mission as
     Participating in the Ecstatic Love of the Triune God*," *Didaskalia* 28 (2017–18): 82.

37   Augustine, *De Trinitate*, 15.31.

38   Anselm K. Min, "Renewing the Doctrine of the Spirit: A Prolegomenon,"
     Perspectives in Religious Studies 19 (1992): 194.

39   Min, "A Prolegomenon," 194.

things…in the intimacy of…divine life" so that God may be all in all (1 Corinthians 15:28).[40]

Thomas Aquinas

In his *Summa Theologica* (*ST*), Thomas Aquinas in large measure carries forward Augustine's understanding of the Holy Spirit as love and gift, quoting frequently from *De Trinitate* to amplify his reasoning. Aquinas begins his exposition on the Holy Spirit by arguing for the Spirit's personhood. He admits that the procession of love within the Trinity "has no proper name of its own," unlike the Son. Nonetheless, citing Augustine, Aquinas first affirms that the Spirit has something in common with the other Persons in the Trinity. Yet, more precisely, the other Persons of the Trinity have something in common with the Holy Spirit—namely, that each is "spirit" and each is "holy." Furthermore, because the Divine Persons proceed within God because of love, the love between the Persons of the Trinity must be a Person as well, "most properly named 'the Holy Spirit.'"[41]

Moving, then, to focus on the nature of Love within the Trinity, Aquinas states that the name Love can be applied to God "essentially and personally." He begins by speaking of the experience of love in human persons: "When anyone loves an object, a certain impression results, so to speak, of the thing loved in the affection of the lover; by reason of which the object loved is said to be in the lover."[42] When love means only the relation within the lover to the thing loved, this can be understood as love applied to God "essentially." Nonetheless, when this love proceeds outward from the person of the lover, it becomes *personal*. If thus applied *personally*, from one Person to another within the Trinity, then this Love is properly named the Holy Spirit "as Word is the proper name of the Son."[43] This Love, moreover, is the love by which the Persons of the Trinity not only love one another, but also

40   Min, "A Prolegomenon," 191.

41   Aquinas, *ST*, I.36.1. Note that the original translation renders the name as Holy Ghost.

42   Aquinas, *ST*, I.37.

43   Aquinas, *ST*, I.37.

love all of creation. Because the Holy Spirit proceeds from the Trinity as love, the Holy Spirit can be rightly called the primary Gift of God "through which all free gifts are given"[44] by God to humanity.

A LOOK AHEAD

This chapter has focused on the emerging understandings of the Holy Spirit in Christian life. In the face of threats to its personhood, its origin, and its status in Christianity, the Holy Spirit has continued to manifest as gift, as love, as relationality, as communion, as grace throughout the centuries to the contemporary age. While various Christian traditions diverge on the Holy Spirit's origin within the mystery of the Trinity—with sometimes regrettable results—the Spirit continues to liberate and re-create human persons individually and collectively through love and grace. As theological reflection on the Holy Spirit continued from the time of Aquinas to the present day, insights associated with the Holy Spirit's presence, action, and influence on individuals and communities spawned new images and insights that complemented those explored in these first two chapters. Some images spring from what may be termed classical approaches to pneumatology, whereas others emerge from what are known as contextual approaches to pneumatology. The distinction between the two approaches will introduce the insights of the next chapter and signals the contextual approach taken in the balance of this book.

FOR REFLECTION

- Of the multiple descriptions of the Spirit in this chapter—love, communion, gift, creativity—which most speaks to your experience? Articulate that experience.
- From your life and prayer, can you add to the ways in which the Spirit might be described?
- How has the love that the Spirit is and gives enlivened and enlightened your life? Share an experience that capsulizes the Spirit's love.

---

44   Aquinas, ST, I.38.

FOR FURTHER READING

Augustine of Hippo. *The Trinity (Works of Saint Augustine: A Translation for the 21st Century)*, ed. John E. Rotelle, OSA; trans. Edmund Hill, OP. Hyde Park, NY: New City Press, 2012.

Grenz, Stanley. "The Holy Spirit: Divine Love Guiding Us Home." *Ex Auditu* 12 (1996): 1–13.

Kotsko, Adam. "Gift and Communio: The Holy Spirit in Augustine's *De Trinitate*." *Scottish Journal of Theology* 64:1 (2011): 1–12.

Ratzinger, Joseph. "The Holy Spirit as *Communio*: Concerning the Relationship of Pneumatology and Spirituality in Augustine." *Communio* 25 (Summer 1998): 324–37.

CHAPTER FOUR

Classical Pneumatologies

Pentecostal and Protestant Perspectives

INTRODUCTION

IN HIS ESSAY "LUTHER and the Holy Spirit: Why Pneumatology Still Matters," Jeffrey Mann claimed the following:

> The person of the Holy Spirit receives little attention in the life of some churches. For many of us, the Spirit is our focus on Pentecost, and we may speak of the Spirit in a vague way when we address the thorny issue of sanctification, but our theology, teaching, and pondering often focus on the other two persons of the Trinity.[1]

Despite Mann's blunt assertion regarding the current state of interest in the Person of the Holy Spirit—one which is echoed by a number of writers in pneumatology—a review of literature over the past fifty years reveals that pneumatology is an idea whose time has come. As Patrick Corcoran observed in his 1979 essay "The Holy Spirit and the Life of the Spirit Today,"

> Within living memory there has been no period…when the Holy Spirit has been so much in the public eye. He has become a superstar—one whose musical has not yet been written—but nonetheless a superstar. People talk

---

1 Jeffrey Mann, "Luther and the Holy Spirit: Why Pneumatology Still Matters," *Currents in Theology and Mission* 34:2 (2007): 111.

and write freely of a New Pentecost, a new Age of the Spirit, the evident signs of the Spirit.[2]

These writings on pneumatology are rooted in a variety of Christian religious traditions—Roman Catholic, Eastern Orthodox, Evangelical, and Pentecostal, among others—and reflect not only the theologians' ecclesial commitment, but also their unique personal and cultural commitments, and thus frequently do not reflect their religious traditions as a whole.

This chapter, as well as the next, focuses principally on the pneumatological insights of theologians who, by and large, approach pneumatology with a classical hermeneutic, that is, theologians who make universal claims concerning the Holy Spirit in relation to the human person.[3] This is not to say that their pneumatologies are not influenced by the particular context of the theologian; rather, for the most part, their pneumatological insights do not principally reflect or respond to the human experiences of a particular community distinguished by gender, race, ethnicity, or culture. Some reflect the specific tradition as a whole, while others reflect the insights of particular theologians within that broader tradition. The theologians whose insights are examined in this chapter are predominantly male, white, European, or North American. These selections are not meant to be exhaustive. Nonetheless, they do offer a representative sampling of the rich fare available in the Christian tradition concerning the liberating action of the Holy Spirit in human life. This banquet begins in this chapter with the Pentecostal and Protestant traditions.

---

2   Patrick Corcoran, C.M., "The Holy Spirit and the Life of the Spirit Today," *Proceedings of the Irish Biblical Association* 3 (1979): 97.

3   The classical or hermeneutic approach reflects the approach of Augustine and Aquinas explored in Chapter Two herein. Within this approach, theologians offer insights and propositions presumed to be universal in scope, and thus applicable to every person in every time and place without distinction.

PENTECOSTAL PNEUMATOLOGIES

There is little doubt that public interest in the Holy Spirit can be traced to the rise of Protestant Pentecostalism.[4] According to Allan Anderson, former Pentecostal minister and leading authority on global Pentecostalism, "The term Pentecostal is appropriate for describing globally all churches and movements that emphasise the workings of the gifts of the Spirit, both on phenomenological grounds and on theological grounds."[5] While there are diverse expressions of Pentecostalism as a whole, often influenced by a diversity of cultures and contexts as it spreads throughout the globe, there are, according to Baptist minister James Purves, certain "indicators" of Pentecostal pneumatology.[6]

Perhaps the most robust indicator of Pentecostalism is the experience of a "direct, non-mediated experience of the Holy Spirit's presence and power."[7] This transformative experience of communion with the Spirit is often associated with an encounter termed Baptism in the Holy Spirit. Most often expressed at the congregational level, Pentecostal pneumatology is conveyed through a sharing of testimonies of how the Spirit is at work to empower individuals through particular events in daily lives. Understood pneumatologically, this power of God in the benefits of Jesus Christ as "Saviour, Healer, Spirit baptiser and Coming King" come to the believer through the Holy Spirit. This points to the fact that the Holy Spirit "comes *from* Jesus Christ as the outpourer of the Holy Spirit; as it also leads *to* Jesus Christ, as the one to whom the Spirit testifies."[8] As a result, the believer is transformed and conformed to Jesus Christ with an empowerment

---

4   Associated with this rise is the emergence of the charismatic movement in the Catholic Church.

5   Allan Anderson, *An Introduction to Pentecostalism* (Cambridge: Cambridge University Press, 2004), 13.

6   Jim Purves, "Water, Fire & Wind: Visiting the Roots of Pentecostal Pneumatology," *Communio Viatorum*, 53:3 (2011): 56.

7   Purves, "Water, Fire & Wind," 57.

8   Purves, "Water, Fire & Wind," 58, emphasis in original.

for mission. As Pentecostal theologian Frank Macchia states, "Spirit baptism empowers, renews, or releases the sanctified life towards outward expression and visible signs of renewal"[9] and initiates the believer "into the deeper dimensions of divine love."[10] This experience of empowerment through the workings of the Holy Spirit is accompanied by human affections, a longing for the Kingdom of God to come in its fullness. Thus, as explained by Pentecostal theologian Kenneth Archer, the experience of the Holy Spirit combines belief, affection, and practice.

> Pentecostal theology must be an integration of *orthopistis* (right belief), *orthopathos* (holy affection), and *orthopraxis* (obedient practice). *Orthopathos* will serve as the interlocutor between *orthopraxis* and *orthopistis* because Pentecostal spirituality manifests as a passionate love for God and compassionate caring for people.[11]

As the link between belief and practice, the affective dimension of the Pentecostal experience of Spirit is more than mere subjective, personal affectivity; it is a sharing in the human affections of Jesus Christ in love for God and longing for the fullness of God's reign inbreaking the present experience of the believer. According to Macchia, this inbreaking of the kingdom into the present experience of believers through the Holy Spirit brings empowerment for Christian living. "The Pentecostal doctrine of the baptism in the Holy Spirit," states Macchia, "at its best can be seen as advocating a kind of 'second conversion,' an awakening to one's vocation in the world and giftings to serve as a witness to Christ."[12]

Macchia's understanding of Spirit baptism for the purpose of

---

9   Frank Macchia, "The Kingdom and the Power," in Michael Welker, ed., *The Work of the Spirit—Pneumatology and Pentecostalism* (Grand Rapids, MI: Eerdmans, 2006), 119.

10 Purves, "Water, Fire & Wind," 60.

11 Kenneth Archer, *The Gospel Revisited: Towards a Pentecostal Theology of Worship and Witness* (Eugene, OR: Pickwick Publications, 2011), 46.

12 Frank Macchia, "Baptised in the Spirit: Reflections in Response to My Reviewers," *Journal of Pentecostal Theology* 16 (2008): 16.

mission and vocation is amplified in the work of Wonsuk Ma, Director of the Oxford Centre for Mission. In his article "'When the Poor are Fired Up': The Role of Pneumatology in Pentecostal-charismatic Mission," Ma points out that "Pentecostal-charismatics represent the 'poor,' for whom poverty and sickness are a part of their lives, and the core of Pentecostal-charismatic pneumatology is 'empowerment' for witness."[13] According to Ma, many of those who embraced Pentecostalism were "poor" in significant ways. Many who took part in the Azusa Street revival[14] were African-Americans and immigrants from the lower economic strata and marginalized from society. As a result, "they understood themselves to be the eager recipients of the Messiah's message of hope, who came 'to preach good news to the poor' under the anointing of the Holy Spirit" (Luke 4: 18).

> These socially "dislocated" found such strong solidarity among themselves, courageously going against commonly accepted social norms such as racial segregation, that they forged a social and spiritual culture where the hope-less found a space to experience God's grace and power. This "haven for the disinherited" created a powerful drawing force to make Pentecostal Christianity a "religion of the poor."[15]

This is significant, Ma contends, because Pentecostalism is "a religion *of* the poor, not *for* the poor."[16] The fact that the Holy Spirit had chosen

---

13 Wonsuk Ma, "'When the Poor are Fired Up': The Role of Pneumatology in Pentecostal-Charismatic Mission," *Transformation* 24:1 (2007): 28.

14 "The Azusa Street Revival was a historic Pentecostal revival meeting that took place in Los Angeles, California and is the origin of the Pentecostal movement. It was led by William J. Seymour, an African American preacher. It began with a meeting on April 14, 1906, and continued until roughly 1915. The revival was characterized by ecstatic spiritual experiences accompanied by miracles, dramatic worship services, speaking in tongues, and inter-racial mingling.... Today, the revival is considered by historians to be the primary catalyst for the spread of Pentecostalism in the 20th century." See "The Azusa Street Revival" at https://www.apostolicarchives.com/articles/article/8801925/173190.htm.

15 Ma, "'When the Poor are Fired Up,'" 29.

16 Ma, "'When the Poor are Fired Up,'" 29.

to manifest among them was liberating and uplifting. Their election moved them from marginalization to ministry, from the Los Angeles revival going forth as missionaries to different parts of the world to present ministries with those who are sick, hungry, and homeless, as well as those in need of inner change and community.[17] As Ma concludes, "If the Pentecostal-charismatic movement can serve this purpose by strengthening and renewing the body of Christ through its healing and restorational potential, its primary historical calling is fulfilled."[18]

PROTESTANT PNEUMATOLOGIES

Beginning this review of Protestant pneumatology requires the admission that the term itself is by no means homogenous. Protestantism is characterized by a multi-faceted nature and development and includes diverse traditions, including Presbyterian, Episcopal, Lutheran, Baptist, Methodist, and Wesleyan. While sometimes used as a synonym for *Protestantism*, the term *Evangelicalism* is more accurately viewed as a movement within Protestant Christianity. Because of this diversity and inclusivity, this section focuses on two specific theologians who have offered liberating pneumatologies from Protestant perspectives: Evangelical theologian Ben Engelbrecht and Reformed theologian Jürgen Moltmann.

Ben Engelbrecht: "The Indwelling Spirit"

More than forty years ago, in his essay "The Indwelling of the Holy Spirit: An Evaluation of Contemporary Pneumatology," Afrikaans theologian Ben Engelbrecht wrote that "Theology today has nothing of greater importance on its agenda than a careful and comprehensive elaboration of the doctrine of the Holy Spirit."[19] In a post-Pentecost, secularized

---

17   Ma, "'When the Poor are Fired Up,'" 30–32.

18   Ma, "'When the Poor are Fired Up,'" 33.

19   Ben Engelbrecht, "The Indwelling of the Holy Spirit, Pt. 1: An Evaluation of Contemporary Pneumatology," *Journal of Theology for Southern Africa* 30 (1980): 19.

world, Engelbrecht contended that "we can only talk *pneumatologically* about God and about any possible experience of God in this world."

> Precisely for this reason, pneumatology today cannot be regarded as only one component of the theological system. It is nothing less than the comprehensive horizon within which, if at all, God-talk can be meaningful and God-experience can become real. The secularized world is the world after pentecost, and after pentecost, the quest for God can only be the quest for the possibility of talking about Him and His presence in the mode and in the power of the Holy Spirit.[20]

Engelbrecht called upon theology to recognize that the Spirit is active beyond the Christian faith and the Church and manifests within the common secular experience of each person. Reflecting insights broadly held across the field of pneumatology and ripened in his South African experience of apartheid, Engelbrecht wrote, "The whole world is [the Spirit's] abode.... The new creation and the Kingdom of God comes...in the wide world itself."[21] He locates the work of the Holy Spirit within the process of world history in which the Spirit is active as liberator and creator of reality.

> God-experience is only conceivable as world-experience, as an experience of the unity of the divine and the human reality in the history of the Holy Spirit with the world. Only in such a new articulation of the doctrine of God, in which pneumatology is not only emphasized but becomes the essence of theology, will theology be able to generate a real experience of faith in man of the twentieth century. It will be a faith within his actual world experience, and theology will then be able to create the conditions in which the relative unity of humanliness, world-experience and God-experience can be expressed.[22]

Rather than characterizing the work of the Spirit as hidden, Engelbrecht conceives the Spirit as "a dynamis, a cosmic and universal

---

20   Engelbrecht, "The Indwelling of the Holy Spirit," 22

21   Engelbrecht, "The Indwelling of the Holy Spirit," 23.

22   Engelbrecht, "The Indwelling of the Holy Spirit," 23.

power," whose essence is "an ongoing actualization of potentialities" that redeems and sanctifies the world.[23]

For Engelbrecht, the essence of pneumatology is captured in the term "Indwelling." Recounted in both testaments of the Bible, the activity of the Holy Spirit indwelling the world increases in intensity, adopts new modes of revelation, and prepares the world for a future of God's own. In this activity, "the Spirit is the new mode of being and activity of Jesus Christ...continuing to make the work which He began during his life on earth effective on a universal scale."[24] The completion of this process, according to Engelbrecht, is the "pneumatizing" of all of creation, which makes human history a history of liberation "in which the real presence of God manifests itself" [25] within the process of political and social liberation.

> [The Holy Spirit] creates a history within history. As the Spirit of change He declares his solidarity with the world. He is present wherever man searches his fellow-man and suffers for him. This is the criterion by which He is known.... Action, not in the form of *praxis pietatis*, but action which changes the world is the way in which the Spirit works.[26]

Jürgen Moltmann: "The Spirit of Life"

By all accounts, Jürgen Moltmann's explicit turn to pneumatology is a relatively recent occurrence. As theologian D. Lyle Dabney notes in his essay "The Advent of the Spirit: The Turn to Pneumatology in the Theology of Jürgen Moltmann," in his early publications, "one is hard pressed to find any sustained, substantive statement concerning the Spirit. Indeed, one writer has commented that pneumatology in Moltmann's early writings is 'simply nonexistent.'"[27] This is con-

---

23   Engelbrecht, "The Indwelling of the Holy Spirit," 24, 25.

24   Engelbrecht, "The Indwelling of the Holy Spirit," 27.

25   Engelbrecht, "The Indwelling of the Holy Spirit," 29.

26   Engelbrecht, "The Indwelling of the Holy Spirit," 30.

27   D. Lyle Dabney, "The Advent of the Spirit: The Turn to Pneumatology in the Theology of Jürgen Moltmann," *The Asbury Theological Journal* 48:1 (1993):

spicuously the case even in Moltmann's work on eschatology, *Theology of Hope*,[28] which, because of its rootedness in Reformation theology, envisions the Spirit as "little more than 'the living remembrance of the living and crucified Christ coupled with a lively hope for the Kingdom,' and precisely for that reason, his theology is left with no connection between the present and the future."[29] Even in his critical work *The Crucified God*,[30] Moltmann's emphasis on the cross as an event between God the Father and God the Son fails to present any developed pneumatology, and thus "Moltmann's portrayal of the Spirit of God remains a *crossless* Spirit, indeed one who stands finally in contradiction to the God of the cross."[31]

In responding to critics of his presentation of the Spirit in *The Crucified God*, Moltmann pointed out the deficit of Western theology as a whole with regard to pneumatology. Describing two models of Trinitarian thought—*Sendungstrinitiit* (a "sending-trinity") and a *Liebestrinitiit* (a "love-trinity")—Moltmann asserts that, in each, the Spirit remains a *passive* object of the *subjective* actions of the Father and the Son. According to Dabney, this realization marks Moltmann's turn to pneumatology,[32] which builds from Moltmann's discussion of the *filioque* in *Trinity and the Kingdom*, to a vision of the Spirit's immanence in the world in *God in Creation*, to emphasis on the mutuality between the Son and the Spirit in *The Way of Jesus Christ*, and, most significantly,

---

81. The writer Dabney cites is Donald A. Claybrook, *The Emerging Doctrine of the Holy Spirit in the Writings of Jürgen Moltmann*, Ph.D. diss., Southern Baptist Theological Seminary, 1983, 185.

28   Jürgen Moltmann, *Theology of Hope: On the Ground and the Implications of a Christian Eschatology* (London: SCM Press, 1967).

29   Dabney, "The Advent of the Spirit," 96, quoting Noel Erskin, from "Christian Hope and the Black Experience," in *Hope for the Church: Moltmann in Dialogue with Practical Theology*, trans. and ed. Theodore Runyon (Nashville, TN: Abingdon, 1979), 126.

30   Jürgen Moltmann, *The Crucified God: The Cross of Christ as the Foundation and Criticism of Christian Theology* (New York: Harper & Row, 1974).

31   Dabney, "The Advent of the Spirit," 98, emphasis in original.

32   Dabney, "The Advent of the Spirit," 100–101.

to a "universal affirmation" in his 1992 volume *The Spirit of Life*.[33] It is from this last work, which Moltmann called "a voyage of discovery into an unknown country,"[34] that this section draws.

From the outset in *Spirit of Life*, Moltmann focuses on the everyday experiences through which persons encounter the Holy Spirit. Rather than asking, "When did you last feel the working of the Holy Spirit?" Moltmann asks, "When were you last conscious of the '*spirit of life*'?"[35] This rephrasing taps the depths of human experience—"our consolations and encouragements."

> 'Spirit' is the love of life which delights us, and the energies of the spirit are the living energies which this love of life awakens in us. The Spirit of God is called *the Holy Spirit* because it makes our life here something living.... The Spirit sets this life in the presence of the living God and in the great river of eternal love.[36]

This understanding of the Holy Spirit goes beyond ecclesiastical institutions, since human beings not only experience the Spirit in the community of church but also "to a much greater degree inwardly, in self-encounter—as the experience that 'God's love has been poured into our hearts through the Holy Spirit'" (Romans 5:5).[37] This experience of God's love is liberating, so people "can get up out of the dust... and no longer have to try despairingly to be themselves."[38] In both verbal and non-verbal expressions, the Spirit "rouses all our senses, permeates the unconscious, ...and quickens the body, giving it new life" (1 Corinthians 6:19f).[39] The Holy Spirit is immanent in human experience, enabling the human spirit to self-transcend in orientation

---

33   Jürgen Moltmann, *The Spirit of Life: A Universal Affirmation* (Minneapolis: Fortress Press, 1992).

34   Moltmann, *The Spirit of Life*, x.

35   Moltmann, *The Spirit of Life*, x.

36   Moltmann, *The Spirit of Life*, x.

37   Moltmann, *The Spirit of Life*, 3.

38   Moltmann, *The Spirit of Life*, 3.

39   Moltmann, *The Spirit of Life*, 3.

toward God. Moreover, the Spirit must be understood as extending beyond the human "as the divine energy of life animating the new creation of all things…in nature, in plants, in animals, and in the ecosystems of the earth." As a result, the *community of creation* is also the *fellowship of the Holy Spirit*, and "the cosmic breadth of God's Spirit… leads to respect for the dignity of all created things, in which God is present through his Spirit."[40]

Thus, it is clear to Moltmann that it is possible for the human person to experience God's Spirit "*in, with, and beneath* each everyday experience of the world,"[41] based on the understanding of the Spirit as the "power of creation and the wellspring of life."[42] Moltmann admits that starting from such everyday experiences of the Holy Spirit in creation often leads to descriptions of the Spirit in non-personal words and phrases—wind, energy, fire, and light. Nonetheless, he asserts, the experience of the Spirit in everyday life is in fact *personal*—a divine indwelling, an inexpressible closeness, a companionship, especially in experiences of suffering. To exemplify this, Moltmann calls upon the Jewish mystical tradition of the Shekinah.[43] In doing so, he amplifies the Shekinah from being understood as a mode of divine presence, to being as a divine counterpart to God, much as Wisdom is seen in scripture. He is able to do so because of the Jewish tradition of the

---

40   Moltmann, *The Spirit of Life*, 9, 10, emphasis in original.

41   Moltmann, *The Spirit of Life*, 34.

42   Moltmann, *The Spirit of Life*, 35.

43   The term *Shekinah* (also spelled *Shekhinah*) is derived from the Hebrew *shakan*, meaning presence or act of dwelling, and is expressed as a feminine gendered substantive. Shekinah appears in a variety of sources including the Talmud, the Midrash, and other post-Biblical rabbinic writings, as well as in the Kabbalah. In the Midrash of the rabbis, the Shekhinah is recognized as an independent divine entity, female in form, who dwells with the chosen in times good or ill, who intercedes compassionately with God for humanity, and who is present even within the humblest circumstances and with the most insignificant of creatures. For a thorough discussion of Shekinah, see Gloria L. Schaab, "The Power of Divine Presence: Toward a *Shekhinah* Christology," in *Christology: Memory, Inquiry, Practice: Proceedings of the College Theology Society 2002*, ed. Anne Clifford and Anthony Godzieba (Maryknoll: Orbis, 2003), 92–115.

Shekinah's earthly companioning of the Jewish people in times of suf-
fering during which the Shekinah intercedes for the suffering with
God, even as the Holy Spirit does for those who suffer (Romans 8:23).
Hence, Moltmann concludes,

> To experience God in all things presupposes that there is a transcendence
> which is immanent in things and which can be inductively discovered. It
> is the infinite in the finite, the eternal in the temporal, and the enduring
> in the transitory.[44]

What, then, is the tangible effect of the Holy Spirit in human life?
According to Moltmann, the Scriptures indicate that people's primary
experience of God is that of "immense liberation—of being set free for
life."[45]

> Inwardly, their energies for living are freed from the obstructions of guilt
> and the melancholy of death. Outwardly, the compulsions of economic,
> political and cultural repression are broken. Inwardly life can be newly
> affirmed. Outwardly new free spaces for living open up.... According to the
> experiences of Israel and according to the experiences of Christian faith,
> the experience of God and the experience of freedom are so deeply fused
> that they belong indissolubly together and become almost synonymous.[46]

Because, however, freedom and liberation tend to arouse protest from
some who warn against too much freedom, and others who wish to
keep the notion of God out of freedom, Moltmann looks at the three
dimensions of faith, hope, and love to explore the true meaning of
freedom in the Spirit: freedom as subjectivity, freedom as sociality,
and freedom as future.

----

44   Moltmann, *The Spirit of Life*, 35.

45   Moltmann, *The Spirit of Life*, 99.

46   Moltmann, *The Spirit of Life*, 99.

LIBERATING FAITH: FREEDOM AS SUBJECTIVITY

According to Moltmann, "personal faith is the beginning of a freedom that renews the whole of life."[47] This is not a freedom defined as self-determination, but rather as "being possessed by the divine energy of life, and participation in that energy."[48] Faith liberates the individual from anxiety and enables one to live in harmony with the Divine. It awakens trust in what is possible and love in places "where death rules." Refusing to be limited by the past, those possessed by the Spirit of God discover their personal subjectivity and seek "the potentialities for life [in oneself and others] which have not yet come."[49] Since "all things are possible for those who believe" (Mark 9:23), believers become "possibility people" who live in the freedom of the Spirit of God.

LIBERATING LOVE: FREEDOM AS SOCIALITY

Moltmann contends that individuals first understand freedom from political history, and this freedom is conceived as *domination*. "Because the whole of history...can be seen as an ongoing struggle for power, the only person who is called free is the victor in this struggle."[50] Nonetheless, freedom can also be understood as *sociality*, the relationships in which, and from which, people live. This freedom is expressed as mutual love.

> It is only in love that human freedom enters its free world. I am free and feel free when I am respected and accepted by other people, and when I for my part respect and accept other people too. I become truly free if I open my life for other people and share it with them, and if other people open their lives for me, and share them with me.[51]

---

47   Moltmann, *The Spirit of Life*, 114.

48   Moltmann, *The Spirit of Life*, 115.

49   Moltmann, *The Spirit of Life*, 115.

50   Moltmann, *The Spirit of Life*, 117.

51   Moltmann, *The Spirit of Life*, 118.

While freedom as domination is destructive of life, freedom as sociality—one with another, one with God, and one with nature—longs for life and heals the wounds inflicted by the struggle for power.

Having explored freedom in the individual subject and in community, Moltmann contends that the freedom that goes beyond each is freedom as *"the creative passion for the possible."*[52] This freedom is directed toward the future coming of the reign of God, characterized as "the limitless kingdom of creative possibilities."[53] Understood as the freedom of determining subjects in relation to a shared vision, liberating hope is more a freedom *for* the future, rather than a freedom *from* the past. Freedom is present where the Spirit is present. Anyone who experiences and lives in the Spirit "lives in the free space of God's creative possibilities, and partakes of them."

> But for that very reason he also participates in the complex web of relationships through which the Creator loves everything he has created, and preserves its life…. But life in…freedom would stagnate in the spider's web of its relationships if it did not as *creative expectation* bring forth projects for the future and thrust beyond reality into the realm of the possible. These three dimensions of freedom are explored through faith, through love, and through hope. In them we correspond in our relationships to the liberating, the social, the coming God.[54]

A LOOK AHEAD

Having surveyed the variety of pneumatological insights in the Pentecostal and Protestant traditions, the next chapter continues this exploration through theologies of the Holy Spirit offered by the Eastern Orthodox and Roman Catholic traditions.

---

52   Moltmann, *The Spirit of Life*, 119, emphasis in original.

53   Moltmann, *The Spirit of Life*, 119.

54   Moltmann, *The Spirit of Life*, 121–22.

FOR REFLECTION

- When were you last conscious of the Spirit of Life "pneumatizing" and "indwelling" all of creation?
- Are you in touch with the Spirit "*in, with, and beneath* each everyday experience of the world?" How would you name that experience?
- Have you experienced the "immense liberation" of the Holy Spirit, "of being set free for life?" Reflect on your experience.

FOR FURTHER READING

Ma, Wonsuk. "'When the Poor are Fired Up': The Role of Pneumatology in Pentecostal-charismatic Mission." *Transformation* 24:1 (2007): 28–34.

Macchia, Frank. "Baptised in the Spirit: Reflections in Response to My Reviewers." *Journal of Pentecostal Theology* 16 (2008): 14–20.

Moltmann, Jürgen. *The Spirit of Life: A Universal Affirmation.* Minneapolis: Fortress Press, 1992.

Purves, Jim. "Water, Fire and Wind: Visiting the Roots of Pentecostal Pneumatology." *Communio Viatorum* 53:3 (2011): 56–73.

CHAPTER FIVE

Classical Pneumatologies

Eastern Orthodox and Roman Catholic Perspectives

INTRODUCTION

THIS CHAPTER TAKES UP the examination of writings on pneumatology rooted in the Eastern Orthodox and Roman Catholic traditions. Like those in the previous chapter, the theologians presented here craft their pneumatologies through universal claims concerning the Holy Spirit in relation to the human person.[1] The presentation of Eastern Orthodox pneumatology reflects the tradition as a whole and is structured thematically according to some of the critical issues raised by theologians in that tradition. Conversely, the wealth of thought in the Roman Catholic tradition is explored through the insights of particular theologians within that broader tradition. These notable theologians, who represent different emphases on the Holy Spirit within the Catholic tradition, include Karl Rahner on the experience of Spirit as grace, Hans Urs von Balthasar on the Spirit as the ecstatic love of God, and Yves Congar on pneumatological anthropology. Once again, this is only a sampling of the riches of these traditions, but it gives a flavor of the liberating action of the Holy Spirit in human life.

---

[1]   The classical approach was motivated by the ideal that truth is best established by the abstraction of concepts rather than grounded in the concrete, real-life situations or contexts of believers around the world.

ORTHODOX PNEUMATOLOGIES

As discussed in Chapter Two, Eastern Orthodoxy holds the Holy Spirit in high regard. From its rejection of the *filioque*, seen as diminishing the equal Personhood of the Holy Spirit, to its affirmation that the energies of the Holy Spirit "govern and transform the world and the activity and will of human beings,"[2] Eastern Orthodoxy asserts the significance of the Spirit in all of history. While the *essence* of the Holy Spirit, like that of the Trinity as a whole, is unfathomable mystery, the Spirit acts with the Persons of the Trinity in history through their *energies*,[3] bringing all of creation and history itself to divine perfection or *theosis*. According to Orthodox theologian Nikos Matsoukas, "there is no gift given to the creature in which the Holy Spirit is not present. The Spirit is the Spirit of truth, the gift of adoption [huiothesia], the promise of future blessings, the first fruits of eternal bliss, a life-giving force, and the source of sanctification."[4] This section explores the activity of the Holy Spirit in creation and human beings in two ways: through the process of theosis and in kenotic hiddenness.

Theosis and the Holy Spirit

One of the primary roles the Holy Spirit enacts in creation and humanity is the process of *theosis*. In his essay "Salvation as Theosis: The Teaching of Eastern Orthodoxy," Donald Fairbairn states, "Probably the central idea of Eastern Orthodox theology is the concept of *theosis*, and Orthodox writers use this Greek word to refer both to humanity's initial vocation… and to salvation."[5] While the English translation of the word as *deification*

---

2   Nikos Matsoukas, "The Economy of the Holy Spirit: The Standpoint of Orthodox Theology," *The Ecumenical Review* 41:3 (1989): 398.

3   The *essence* of the Divine refers to God's very nature, which is shrouded in mystery and inaccessible to humanity. The *energies*, on the other hand, refer to the ways in which the Divine works in the world, the Presence of God in creation, His presence among us and in us, what God is doing in and for creation. Thus, God is both wholly transcendent in mystery, while truly immanent in history.

4   Matsoukas, "The Economy of the Holy Spirit," 399.

5   Donald Fairbairn, "Salvation as Theosis: The Teaching of Eastern Orthodoxy,"

gives some people pause, Fairbairn clarifies the fact that this does not translate to an ontological identification with God. Rather, its meaning corresponds to what other traditions term sanctification or communion with God. The means by which persons undergo this process of *theosis* or sanctification is through the grace of the Holy Spirit.

According to theologian Vladimir Lossky, "The Son has become like us by the incarnation; we become like Him by deification, by partaking of the divinity in the Holy Spirit."[6] Eastern Orthodoxy teaches that it is only in the Spirit that persons are transformed into the likeness of God through grace. While such grace is uncreated—that is, of the essence of God—it is communicated through the divine energies, principally through the sacraments and through human striving.

Christophoros Stavropoulos writes that "the Christian life comes into being with the sacraments—principally Baptism, Penance, and Eucharist—and with holy works, those virtuous works which are done with a pure and holy motive in the name of Christ."[7] The Eucharist exemplifies the supreme means of *theosis* since, in the Eucharist, people become united with and as the Body of Christ. Hence, a principal locus of deification is the Church. Constituted by the Spirit, the Church "is a living organism and hence the tradition is a living witness, not just a harmony with the past but a principle of live progress, growth, regeneration and reformation."[8] It is the locus in which the charisms of human persons are called forth and actualized, the living body through which persons attain full dignity in communion with the Holy Spirit.

Nonetheless, while the Holy Spirit is active in the Church, the Church does not control the Spirit or dispense the gift of grace in and of itself. As theologian John Meyendorff maintains, "It is not the church which, through the medium of its institutions, bestows the Holy Spirit, but it is the Spirit which validates every aspect of church life, including

---

Themelios 23:3 (1998): 42.

6   Vladimir Lossky, *In the Image and Likeness of God*, ed. J.H. Erickson (Crestwood, NY: St Vladimir's Seminary Press [hereafter SVS], 1974), 109.

7   Christophoros Stavropoulos, *Partakers of the Divine Nature*, trans. S. Harakas (Minneapolis: Light and Life Publishing Co., 1976), 32.

8   Matsoukas, "The Economy of the Holy Spirit," 402.

the institutions."[9] The Church exists in order to promote the deification of its members. However, deification also comes about through
the grace of the Holy Spirit active in human works. While this does not
mean that human beings can merit deification through their works,
good works such as prayer, fasting, and service to others represent
humanity's participation in the process of deification. As Matsoukas
notes, "Human beings as creatures made in the image and likeness of
God and at the same time in the image and likeness of the universe are
obliged to become fellow-workers with God by displaying his creative
activity."[10]

  This emphasis on human partaking in the process of *theosis* is made
clear in the striking words of Vladimir Lossky: "God becomes power-
less before human freedom; he cannot violate it since it flows from his
own omnipotence. Certainly man was created by the will of God alone;
but he cannot be deified by it alone."[11] In divine respect for human
freedom, the Holy Spirit requires the participation of each person
in his/her deification. Thus, "the process of deification is the result
of both the Holy Spirit's action, performed by means of the church's
sacraments, and of human effort to acquire virtue."[12] Moreover, it is a
process that is not complete even in death, since the fullness of *theosis* comes at the eschaton. Thus, prayers for those who have died have
a significant place in Orthodox piety and liturgy, since such prayer
assists the departed in the ongoing process of deification.

Kenosis and the Spirit

Despite the prominence of the Holy Spirit in creation and human life,
"It is something of an unofficial dogma in Orthodox theology," states
theologian Jeffrey Vogel, "that the Holy Spirit is not manifested personally in the economy of salvation, but is rather the divine person

---

9   John Meyendorff, *Catholicity and the Church* (Crestwood, NY: SVS, 1983), 28.

10   Matsoukas, "The Economy of the Holy Spirit," 404.

11   Vladimir Lossky, *Orthodox Theology: An Introduction*, trans. I. Kasarcodi-Watson
     (Crestwood, NY: SVS, 1978), 73.

12   Fairbairn, "Salvation as Theosis," 45.

who does the manifesting, who reveals Christ to the world."[13] This understanding of the Spirit has been articulated by terms such as the self-effacement, the unselfing, the hiddenness, the concealment, the transparency, or the kenosis of the Holy Spirit, all designed to communicate that the Holy Spirit reveals the Divine—or more precisely Christ—but is yet unseen. As New Testament scholar John Breck contends:

> If the Spirit is viewed as other than the Spirit of God and the Spirit of Christ, personally distinct from the Father and the Son yet essentially united with them, then we do violence to God's self-revelation.... The Spirit, then, is not some independent, autonomous charismatic power...acting upon its own authority. His will and operation are one with the will and operation of the Father and the Son.[14]

While Breck's contention must be carefully parsed so as not to diminish the unique Personhood of the Holy Spirit, it is representative of the so-called "unofficial dogma in Orthodox theology" pointed out by Vogel in his exposition on "how the Spirit hides." As Breck himself states the issue, "the 'face' or personal identity of God the Father is revealed by the Son, whereas the 'face' of the Son is revealed to us by the Spirit. But the Spirit himself has no other divine person to make him known. Does he indeed have a face, a personal identity?"[15] Responses to this question have resulted in "pneumatological Christologies" that contend that the Spirit constitutes and communicates the mystery of Christ. However, Breck himself advances a "Christological pneumatology" in which "the mystery of the Spirit is revealed, constituted and communicated by Jesus, the Son of God."[16]

Retrieving texts that speak of the Spirit's activity in both the Jewish and Christian Testaments, Breck crafts a pneumatology centered on

---

13 Jeffrey A. Vogel, "How the Spirit Hides: Rival Conceptions in Recent Orthodox Theology," *St Vladimir's Theological Quarterly* 53:1 (2009): 99.

14 John Breck, "'The Lord is Spirit:' An Essay in Christological Pneumatology," *The Ecumenical Review* 42:2 (1990): 114–15.

15 John Breck, "The Face of the Spirit," *PRO ECCLESIA* III:2 (1994): 166.

16 Breck, "The Face of the Spirit," 167.

the Spirit as "the mode of God's loving, blessing and saving presence among the remnant of Israel"[17] and as "Revealer, Teacher, Defender, Sanctifier, and Giver of Life"[18] in the Gospels and Epistles. He concludes from the former sources that the Spirit is the vehicle of God's self-revelation through inspiration, and from the latter that "the face of the Spirit, then, is none other than the face of Jesus; yet the Spirit remains the 'other Paraclete' (John 14:16f.), intimately united with the Son, yet personally distinct from him."[19]

Breck is not alone in drawing such a conclusion. It is echoed in that of theologian and patriarch Kallistos Ware, who suggests that the Spirit is *transparent*: "Just as the air remains itself invisible to us but acts as the medium through which we see and hear other things, so the Spirit does not reveal to us his own face, but shows us always the face of Christ."[20] Such transparency is a form of *kenosis* for theologian John Meyendorff, who writes, "The role of the Spirit in salvation (as also in the internal life of the Trinity) is 'kenotic': it is always directed to the Other."[21] This notion of kenosis is also advanced by theologian Vladimir Lossky, who states:

> The divine Persons do not themselves assert themselves, but one bears witness to another. It is for this reason that St John Damascene said that "the Son is the image of the Father, and the Spirit the image of the Son." It follows that the third Hypostasis of the Trinity is the only one not having His image in another Person. The Holy Spirit, as Person, remains unmanifested, hidden, concealing Himself in His very appearing.[22]

These assertions may be unsatisfying for those who yearn to identify the Spirit with a unique identity and Personhood all the Spirit's

---

17   Breck, "The Face of the Spirit," 167–69.

18   Breck, "The Face of the Spirit," 169–74.

19   Breck, "The Face of the Spirit," 173.

20   Kallistos Ware, *The Orthodox Way* (Crestwood, NY: SVS Press, 2002), 91.

21   Meyendorff, *Catholicity and the Church*, 25.

22   Vladimir Lossky, *The Mystical Theology of the Eastern Church* (Crestwood, NY: SVS Press, 1998), 160.

own. An alternative perspective on the kenosis of the Holy Spirit has been offered by Orthodox theologian Sergius Bulgakov. While Bulgakov agrees that the Spirit is kenotically unmanifested in the economy, he interprets that event differently as a "self-limitation" or "attenuation" of the Spirit's energies so as to dwell with and not overwhelm finite creatures; "the Spirit's hiddenness is less a result of the other-directed nature of the third hypostasis, and more the consequence of restraint."[23]

Identifying the self-limitation of the Spirit with that of the Divine in creation as a whole, Bulgakov explains that the Spirit diminishes divine power in relation to creatures to preserve such limited creatures in being. Since creation is in the process of becoming toward fullness and has not yet reached the fullness of being, the Spirit, although "the force of being and the giver of life," limits divine power "in conformity with the condition of the latter,"

> for otherwise creation would be abolished, would return to its original nonbeing. The Father, in sending the Spirit in the creative "let there be" restrains the Spirit's force and fullness, as it were—if only by the fact that he manifests them in time, in becoming.[24]

The reality of creature finitude is not the only condition that results in the kenosis of the Spirit. Bulgakov also points out that the kenosis of the Spirit's power in creation "remains limited by the measure of creaturely reception.... [The] synergism of grace with creaturely freedom leads to such a self-limitation."[25] Hence, the Spirit adapts the divine self to the capacity of creatures to receive the Spirit. Vogel conceives of this as "a gracious self-limitation on the part of the Spirit,"[26] even as the Spirit continues the divine activity of creation.

How might Orthodox pneumatology be liberating for Christian life? While Bulgakov offers an interpretation of the Spirit's kenosis

---

23 Vogel, "How the Spirit Hides," 109.

24 Sergius Bulgakov, *The Comforter*, trans. Boris Jakim (Grand Rapids, MI: Eerdmans, 2004), 220.

25 Sergius Bulgakov, *The Bride of the Lamb*, trans. Boris Jakim (Grand Rapids, MI: Eerdmans, 2002), 398.

26 Vogel, "How the Spirit Hides," 111.

that emphasizes divine power and glory, Vogel suggests that this is a misconception of the Spirit's movement. For the Spirit is "the one who proceeds from the Father, the one who scatters and is poured out, drives and sheds abroad, in short, the one who is essentially out-go-ing"[27] rather than self-limiting. Hence, like the majority of Orthodox theologians cited above, Vogel opts for a meaning of kenosis as "oth-er-centeredness," and in this is the liberating energy of the Spirit.

> The Spirit is the one by whom men and women are driven beyond them-selves, hidden...because he works within and underneath the believer in Christ. The Spirit's hiddenness is an essential aspect of his role in facil-itating the attention of one to another.... For it is only in "really seeing" another person that I am able to love him, only in recognizing his "absolute otherness" that he becomes more to me than an object of my imagination or will. If so, the hiddenness of the Spirit is not a problem to be solved, but the very source of the communion of saints.[28]

ROMAN CATHOLIC PNEUMATOLOGIES

This section presents the diverse pneumatologies of three premier theologians in the Roman Catholic tradition: German Jesuit Karl Rahner, Swiss priest Hans Urs von Balthasar, and French Dominican Yves Congar.

Karl Rahner: "The Experience of the Spirit as Grace"

In his book *Karl Rahner: Theologian of the Graced Search for Meaning*,[29] Geffrey Kelly explores the reality of the presence and action of the Holy Spirit reflected in specific works of theologian Karl Rahner. Describing Rahner as a "spirit-driven, prayerful religious person whose theological reflections have helped to make it possible for the

---

27   Vogel, "How the Spirit Hides," 122.

28   Vogel, "How the Spirit Hides," 122.

29   Geffrey B. Kelly, ed., *Karl Rahner: Theologian of the Graced Search for Meaning* (Minneapolis: Augsburg Fortress, 1992).

Church to become more truly a pastoral community serving people of all cultures in the modern world," Kelly focuses on Rahner's belief in the "everyday experience of God" in and through the Holy Spirit.[30] Graced by the sending of the Spirit, who "symbolizes every facet of the interrelatedness of creator with creature," the created world is the "sphere of God's caring, compassionate presence."[31] Because of this, the Spirit is not confined to the institution of the Church, but equally "touches individual persons, moving them...to the discovery of God in the inner moments of their being more fully human and being in relationships that are caring and unselfish."[32] This is clearly expressed in Rahner's own description of the instances of the Spirit:

> Wherever there is selfless love, wherever duties are carried out without hope of reward, wherever the incomprehensibility of death is calmly accepted, wherever people are good with no hope of reward; in all these instances the Spirit is experienced, even though a person may not dare give this interpretation to the experience.[33]

While there are many ways to approach Rahner's pneumatology, theologian Francis J. Caponi contends that it is most consistent to do so "with Rahner's own intentions...primarily in terms of his formidable theology of grace."[34] Rooted in Rahner's broader understanding of the "supernatural existential," the graced action of the Holy Spirit is integral to the insistent movement and insatiable yearning of human persons in self-transcendent openness toward God. Human persons in their everyday existence experience "a deeper reality, the longing

---

30 Geffrey B. Kelly, "The Everyday Experience of God: Karl Rahner's Theology of the Holy Spirit," *The Living Pulpit* 5:1 (1996): 35.

31 Kelly, "The Everyday Experience of God," 35.

32 Kelly, "The Everyday Experience of God," 35.

33 Karl Rahner, "How Is the Holy Spirit Experienced Today?" in *Karl Rahner in Dialogue: Conversations and Interviews, 1965–1982*, ed. Paul Imhof and Hubert Biallowons; trans. Harvey D. Egan (New York: Crossroad, 1986), 142.

34 Francis J. Caponi, "Aspects of the Pneumatologies of Karl Rahner and Hans Urs von Balthasar," *New Theology Review* 20:1 (2007): 10.

for more,"[35] in and through their finite existence, which Rahner terms "categorical reality." According to Rahner, the nature of the human person, as the very essence of transcendence, "pushes on past every finite thing and relationship...and transcends toward that which has no limits."[36]

> Humans want more: not some degree of beauty but the fullness of beauty; not some degree of existence but existence itself. This is our "transcendental" dimension, that is, our fundamental longing...for more. We are open to and truly satisfied by nothing less than the divine.[37]

Possessing an orientation to boundless mystery, the human person is satisfied by nothing less than God, and the context in which any reflection on the Holy Spirit must begin is the awareness of "the Spirit as the gift in which God bestows God's self on human beings."[38]

Rahner roots his reflection on the Holy Spirit in the Bible, without which persons could not comprehend their own experience of Spirit. However, because the Biblical understanding of the Holy Spirit is rooted in the *personal* experience of the early Christians, "we are especially entitled to ask where and how we experience the Spirit in our own selves in this personal, Biblical way."[39] To do so, Rahner states, one must recognize that the experience of Spirit is "incommensurable" with ordinary experiences of everyday life. Rather, the experience of Spirit is one which human beings have within themselves, "a unique, original basic experience which always remains hidden behind all the specific objective experiences of that same being."[40] Because of this, one may wonder if there is a way to validate experiences of Spirit within oneself. And, says Rahner, there is indeed.

---

35   Caponi, "Aspects," 12.

36   Karl Rahner, "Experience of the Holy Spirit," in Kelly, *Karl Rahner*, 226.

37   Caponi, "Aspects," 11.

38   Karl Rahner, "Experience of the Holy Spirit," in Kelly, *Karl Rahner*, 220.

39   Rahner, "Experience of the Holy Spirit," 221.

40   Rahner, "Experience of the Holy Spirit," 222.

To authenticate experience of the Holy Spirit, Rahner begins with the testimony of the mystics who report their personal experiences of grace as the direct presence of and union with God in the Spirit "in the sacred night, or in a blessed illumination, in a void silently filled by God.... And that that experience is the 'experience of the Holy Spirit.'"[41] Although "normal Christians" might feel that such experiences do not concern them, the testimony of the mystics authenticates experiences that every Christian and every human being can have. Even if one does not see oneself as a mystic, "That experience *is* given to us, even though we usually overlook it in pursuit of our everyday lives…and do not take it seriously enough."[42] Such experiences are boundless; whatever one is aware of in one's everyday consciousness is "only a minute isle…in a boundless ocean of nameless mystery" that we call God.[43]

> The mystery pure and simple that we call God is not a special, particularly unusual piece of objective reality, something to be added to and included in the other realities of our naming and classifying experience. God is the comprehensive though never comprehended ground and presupposition of our experience and of the objects of that experience.[44]

Even if one cannot parse the difference between the experience itself and the experience of God within it, God dwells within the "unnamed and unsignposted" expanse of consciousness. As Rahner emphasizes, "Transcendental experience, even when and where it is mediated through an actual categorical object, is always divine experience in the midst of everyday life."[45]

So, how might one recognize this experience of the infinite Spirit of God if it is so enmeshed with finite experience? Rahner suggests that there are some experiences which, because of their positive nature, because of "the magnitude and glory, goodness, beauty, and

---

41 Rahner, "Experience of the Holy Spirit," 223.

42 Rahner, "Experience of the Holy Spirit," 225.

43 Rahner, "Experience of the Holy Spirit," 226.

44 Rahner, "Experience of the Holy Spirit," 227.

45 Rahner, "Experience of the Holy Spirit," 228.

illumination of our individual experiential reality promise and point to eternal light and everlasting life."[46] However, while such positive transcendental experiences exist, many times experiences of glory and goodness occur as contrast experiences. They emerge to counter human experiences of void, of failure, and of darkness, liberating persons from that which threatens to engulf them. Hence to clarify what he means by experiences of Spirit, Rahner recounts a variety of actual life events in which one finds the Holy Spirit of God.

> There is the man who discovers that he can forgive though he receives no reward for it.... There is a woman who is really good to another woman from whom no echo of understanding and thankfulness is heard in return.... There is one who is silent although he could defend himself, although he is unjustly treated.... One could go on like this forever, perhaps even without coming to that experience which for this or that man or woman is the experience of the Spirit, freedom, and grace in his or her life.[47]

As difficult as such experiences are, it is here in which persons find the experience of the Holy Spirit—in the contrast, in the experience of liberation from the quotidian and the exceptional experiences of life which often burden and oppress.

> ...where responsibility in freedom is still accepted and borne where it has no apparent offer of success or advantage,

> ....where the sum of all accounts of life, which no one can calculate alone, is understood by an incomprehensible other as good, though it still cannot be "proven,"

> ....where we rehearse our own deaths in everyday life, and try to live in such a way as we would like to die, peaceful and composed...there is God and God's liberating grace. There we find what we Christians call the Holy Spirit of God.[48]

---

46   Rahner, "Experience of the Holy Spirit," 228.

47   Rahner, "Experience of the Holy Spirit," 229–30.

48   Rahner, "Experience of the Holy Spirit," 231.

Rahner encourages women and men to find this experience in their own lives and to recognize it clearly as an experience of the Holy Spirit. He urges persons to embrace a "mysticism in everyday life" beyond institutionalism, where the offer of God's liberating grace is offered to all persons, Christians and non-Christians alike. Seeking the experience of the Spirit and of grace in one's own life, one can find the Spirit only in self-forgetfulness, only in the search for God, only in generous love for others. "If we release ourselves to this experience of Spirit... then...the Holy Spirit is actually at work in us. Then the hour of the Spirit's grace has come."[49]

Hans Urs von Balthasar: "Spirit as the Ecstatic Love of God"

In contrast to many of the theologians discussed thus far, Hans Urs von Balthasar never taught theology in university and never viewed theology as fundamentally academic.[50] In his article *"Deus Semper Major—Ad Majorem Dei Gloriam*: The Pneumatology and Spirituality of Hans Urs Von Balthasar," theologian John Sachs states that, for Balthasar, "theology is first and foremost the loving contemplation of faith upon the personal Word which God has spoken to the world in Jesus Christ.... Therefore, theology as an activity of faith must not be separated from spirituality."[51] According to Sachs, the bridge between Balthasar's theology and spirituality is pneumatology. "The Spirit [for Balthasar] is the divine witness and infallible interpreter throughout history of the truth of the Christ event."[52] The Spirit enables believers to grasp the divine love that has grasped them in the paschal mystery and in the ongoing activity of God in history. Moreover, the Holy Spirit reveals this God as "'ever-greater,' radically free and ever-new."[53]

---

49   Rahner, "Experience of the Holy Spirit," 233.

50   John R. Sachs, *"Deus Semper Major—Ad Majorem Dei Gloriam*: The Pneumatology and Spirituality of Hans Urs von Balthasar," *Gregorianum* 74:4 (1993): 631.

51   Sachs, *"Deus Semper Major,"* 631.

52   Sachs, *"Deus Semper Major,"* 638.

53   Sachs, *"Deus Semper Major,"* 632.

In his writing on the Trinity, Balthasar identifies the Holy Spirit as "the unknown lying behind the Word,"[54] the one who reveals God as ever-greater mystery, as divine freedom in the infinite fullness of love. The Spirit "is like the light that cannot be seen except upon the object that is lit up; and he is the love between the Father and the Son that has appeared in Jesus."[55] According to Balthasar, this divine love is not static, but, as revealed by the Holy Spirit, is *"ever-greater* love.*"*

> It is true that God is always more than what a human, even in eternal bliss, could grasp. But God, even though perfectly luminous and clear is also the ever greater One to God's own self: that "excess" which expresses itself personally above all in the Holy Spirit.[56]

Balthasar asserts that the love between the Father and the Son is what brings forth the Holy Spirit as "the ever-greater 'more' of their love," more than the "we" of the two who love. The love between the two persons of the Trinity is not self-contained or exclusive, according to Balthasar; rather, this love is creative, bringing forth a new life that is truly an "Other," the Person of the Holy Spirit.

> [The] divine Spirit as the "Third Person" comes forth from this fellowship as the miracle of eternal fruitfulness…ineffably welling forth from the common "breath" (pneuma) of their mutual indwelling…a mysterious Someone of his own: one who is between them and denotes and seals this unity, precisely because he is this unity in a personal manner…. God as Spirit is absolute…poured-out totality of being: as love.[57]

As the "love of the Father and the Son objectified as a Person… pouring forth into infinity,"[58] the Holy Spirit represents *"the sovereign*

---

54   Hans Urs von Balthasar, *Creator Spirit* (San Francisco: Ignatius Press, 1993), 105ff.

55   Balthasar, *Creator Spirit*, 111.

56   Hans Urs von Balthasar, *Theodramatik IV* (Einsiedeln: Johannes Verlag, 1983), 68.

57   Balthasar, *Creator Spirit*, 107.

58   Balthasar, *Creator Spirit*, 107.

freedom of God in person."[59] The Spirit "is the ultimate divine freedom that is the fruit of the union of Father and Son…and, as this 'We,' [the Spirit] is once again the absolute truth of God, the disclosure of the eternal life of the divine love."[60] In the Spirit, the love of God has a boundless future, alive and always new. Nonetheless, this love, while ever-new, is not different from the original love between the Persons of the Trinity from which the Spirit emerges. Rather, the Spirit makes known the love of God in novel and surprising forms in response to creations and its creatures. Thus, while "The Spirit never lets 'his divine freedom blow elsewhere than in the sphere of the love between Father and Son,'…as this love is bottomless, there are always new directions in which he is able to go."[61]

This fullness of love is pre-eminently revealed in the life and mission, cross, and resurrection of Jesus Christ. Jesus is the one who is sent into the world as a sign of the love that characterizes the Trinity within and who incarnates this mutual love as "a being for the other."[62] The fruit of this "being for the other" who continues to communicate the total, mutual love of the Trinity is the Holy Spirit. Balthasar contends that the life and mission of Jesus of Nazareth was shaped and animated by the Holy Spirit, to whom he was receptive and obedient. "The Father's great love for the world, the love that has sent us his Son, enters into the world and history as an event brought about by the Holy Spirit."[63] It is the Spirit who overshadowed Mary at his conception, who descended upon Jesus in the Jordan, who drove him into the wilderness, who disclosed to him his mission. Moreover, "What the Spirit has established is a reality that necessarily remains in him: the total human existence of Jesus on earth is an existence and mission in

---

59   Sachs, "*Deus Semper Major*," 642.

60   Balthasar, *Creator Spirit*, 127, emphasis in original.

61   Jeffrey A. Vogel, "The Unselfing Activity of the Holy Spirit in the Theology of Hans Urs von Balthasar," *LOGOS* 10:4 (2007): 20; internal quote from Balthasar, *Creator Spirit*, 156.

62   Sachs, "*Deus Semper Major*," 640.

63   Balthasar, *Creator Spirit*, 118.

the Holy Spirit."[64] This reality is most clearly articulated in the Gospel of Luke, in which Jesus quotes the words of the prophet Isaiah:

> The Spirit of the Lord is upon me,
> because he has anointed me
> to bring good news to the poor.
> He has sent me to proclaim release to the captives
> and recovery of sight to the blind,
> to let the oppressed go free,
> to proclaim the year of the Lord's favor.
> (Lk 4: 18–19)

In his unfolding life in mission, the Spirit "who is present in Jesus is the absolute and inflexible rule for him, which demands absolute obedience.... [The] Spirit is for Jesus the power in which he trusts in all his weakness."[65]

While "as earthly man, [Jesus] is obedient to the Spirit; exalted, he breathes the Spirit into the world. So he can cause believers to share in both obeying the Spirit and communicating the spirit, essential roles for the members of the Church of Jesus."[66] Thus, Francis Caponi concludes, "The relationship of the Christian to the Spirit imitates that of Christ."[67] Like Jesus, as a disciple on mission, the Christian must be open, attentive, and obedient to the Spirit who in prayer discloses God's desires for each person in a union of freedom and obedience. In a "relationship of 'mutual existence in,'" the Christian "lives in the realm of the Pneuma, and the Pneuma lives in believers."[68] In the Spirit, "the sphere of the love of the Father is opened up for [all], the love that has borne witness to itself through the Son." The Christian is called to this sphere of love and "invited to exist in it."[69]

---

64   Balthasar, *Creator Spirit*, 119.

65   Balthasar, *Creator Spirit*, 120.

66   Hans Urs von Balthasar, *Theo-Drama: Theological Dramatic Theory, Vol. II*, trans. Graham Harrison (San Francisco: Ignatius Press, 1992), 259.

67   Caponi, "Aspects," 10.

68   Balthasar, *Creator Spirit*, 131.

69   Balthasar, *Creator Spirit*, 131.

As the one who forms the existence in mission of the believer, the Spirit exercises utter freedom in shaping the Christian life. Communicating this freedom entails a dialogue between God and the believer in and through the Holy Spirit. "The heart of such prayer," Sachs maintains, "is the necessity to live in open self-surrender before God, ready and willing to receive the Spirit and to be sent with a concrete mission to fulfill." As an artist is freed when the idea for a new creation takes possession of him or her, so the Christian is freest when grasped by the Spirit, when living in openness and responsiveness to the Spirit's promptings.

> At its root, life in the Spirit is a contemplative, obedient receptivity vis-à-vis the absolutely free God. But, it is at the same time existence in active, creative mission, in which the individual experiences both the liberation and fulfillment of his or her own finite existence and the call to join God in God's on-going engagement in the world through the Spirit.[70]

To the extent that the Christian is able to do so, "he or she will be able to live and act in the spontaneity of the infinitely free Spirit at work within...[with] the desire to serve and the readiness to be sent: *contemplativus in actione*." In the Spirit, "human freedom is liberated and fulfilled in the freedom of God."[71]

Yves Congar: "Pneumatological Anthropology"

At the outset of his meditation on the Holy Spirit, Yves Congar observed, "The Spirit is without a face and almost without a name. He is the wind who is not seen, but who makes things move. He is known by his effects."[72] Moreover, Congar believed it was more important for people to live in the Holy Spirit than to try to construct an adequate theology of the Holy Spirit.[73] Nonetheless, Congar's pneumatology is a force to be reckoned with, especially against the backdrop of the

---

70 Sachs, "*Deus Semper Major*," 654.

71 Sachs, "*Deus Semper Major*," 653, 654.

72 Yves Congar, *I Believe in the Holy Spirit* (New York: Seabury, 1983), III:144.

73 Congar, *I Believe in the Holy Spirit*, I:x.

ecclesiological pneumatologies of the nineteenth and early twentieth centuries in which "the Holy Spirit is not even mentioned."[74] As
theologian Elizabeth Groppe notes, "This is not to say that the Roman
Catholic theology of this period had no operative pneumatology at all.
From the 1880s through the 1950s, Catholic theology devoted much
attention to the indwelling of the Spirit in the human soul."[75]

Congar bemoaned the separation of spiritual anthropology from
ecclesiology that followed the patristic period. "Maintaining the
proper balance between the Spirit who gives life to the Church and
the breath of God in individual believers demands that these two
aspects not become confused nor completely separated."[76] Hence,
Congar presents a "pneumatological anthropology" inseparable
from "pneumatological ecclesiology."[77] In keeping with the focus of
this text, nevertheless, this section will hew as closely as possible to
Congar's "pneumatological anthropology," the Holy Spirit in personal
lives. It does so with the clear understanding that "at all costs, Congar
wants to avoid proposing any kind of individualistic pneumatological
anthropology."[78]

Grounding his reflections in the Biblical teaching of the *imago Dei*,
Congar understood the human person as a "being-toward" the other.
Human fulfillment, therefore, is solely in communion and love for one
another in response to an "in-built capacity to being called by God."[79]

> The Holy Spirit dwells within men's hearts, at the very center of their being,
> and becomes himself their innermost inclination, their natural tendency.

---

74   Congar, *I Believe in the Holy Spirit*, II:92.

75   Elizabeth Teresa Groppe, "The Contribution of Yves Congar's Theology of the
     Holy Spirit," *Theological Studies* 62 (2001): 453. I owe a debt of gratitude to Dr.
     Groppe for her excellent elucidation of Congar's thought.

76   Mark E. Ginter, "The Holy Spirit and Morality: A Dynamic Alliance," in "An
     Ecumenical Colloquium on Yves Congar," *CTSA Proceedings* 51 (1996): 170.

77   Groppe, "Congar's Theology of the Holy Spirit," 457.

78   Ginter, "The Holy Spirit and Morality," 169.

79   Groppe, "Congar's Theology of the Holy Spirit," 457; Congar, "L'homme est
     capable d'être appelé," *Vie spirituelle* 120 (1969): 391.

Himself immutable and unique, he is the living master of the impulse he imparts to each and makes all things converge upon that unity which is the proper outcome of his presence, for he is love.[80]

Congar augmented his emphasis on relationality with an emphasis on human freedom. Human beings in the power of the Holy Spirit choose both this mutuality with others and receptivity to God. Nonetheless, for Congar, "The highest degree of freedom is not to govern oneself, but to be wholly governed by God."

> [While] God is outside and above us, he also dwells within us. Because he is God, he is in some sense within us physically; spiritually and morally he is within us through the free gift of his Holy Spirit "in our hearts" (Gal. 4:6). Thus it is from within, gently, that he moves us towards what is good, to the true good. The pressure or attraction under whose influence we act is the Holy Spirit himself.[81]

Congar clearly recognizes that this movement toward the true good has been diverted by human sinfulness. Within this state of conflict and division, however, "the Holy Spirit works, inwardly perfecting our spirit by communicating to it a new dynamism, and this functions so well that man refrains from evil through love."[82] Thus, the indwelling Holy Spirit "who is Good and Love"[83] continues to advance and attract persons until "we love God with the very love with which God loves us."[84]

Congar's insights in this regard clearly echo those of his fellow theologians Rahner and Balthasar. Moreover, like them, Congar states that the goal of the Spirit's action within human beings moves persons

---

80 Yves Congar, "The Call to Ecumenism and the Work of the Holy Spirit," in *Dialogue Between Christians: Catholic Contributions to Ecumenism*, trans. Philip Loretz, 100–106 (Westminster, MD: Newman Press, 1966), 102.

81 Yves Congar, "Holy Spirit and Spirit of Freedom," in *Laity, Church and World*, trans. Donald Attwater, 1–34 (London: Geoffrey Chapman, 1960), 14.

82 Congar, *I Believe in the Holy Spirit*, II:125.

83 Congar, *I Believe in the Holy Spirit*, II:126.

84 Groppe, "Congar's Theology of the Holy Spirit," 459.

not simply to an amorphous "good," but, specifically, a good that "corresponds to...what Christ must be and do in us."[85] For Congar, such development into Christ is inevitably expressed and fulfilled in the Church, since "[e]cclesial life is both an expression of our new life in the Spirit and a means toward our transfiguration, for our fulfillment as creatures made in the divine image can be found only in communion with God and with others."[86] Hence, for Congar, pneumatology is more than "a profound analysis of the indwelling of the Holy Spirit in individual souls."[87] It must include a "pneumatological ecclesiology," the means through which Christians are graced with the Holy Spirit in word, sacrament, and ministry within the Church. Moreover, the Holy Spirit builds up the Church through the charisms which, with the Spirit, grace believers. As Groppe states, "The Spirit awakens natural human talents—gifts for teaching, preaching, artistry, music, healing, justice advocacy, reconciliation, peace-making, and so forth—and elevates them to a new level of orientation toward God in the love and service of others."[88] In so doing, the Holy Spirit fosters communion, not conformity, "by respecting and even stimulating their diversity."[89] In this is both relation and liberation.

> The Holy Spirit is the sun of the soul and, at the same time, the wind "blowing where it will" (John 3:8), sowing the seed of its choice where no human hand has planted. He is also the life-thrust urging on its growth and he provides the soil to nourish it. The work and the mark of the Holy Spirit can be recognized by the fact that the [people] who do not know one another, or many various and apparently haphazard circumstances, should come together in the performance of some spiritual work in building up the Body of Christ. For it is in this way that [the Spirit] works.[90]

---

85   Yves Congar, *The Mystery of the Temple*, trans. R.E. Trevett (Westminster, MD: Newman Press, 1962), 154, emphasis in original.

86   Groppe, "Congar's Theology of the Holy Spirit," 460.

87   Congar, *I Believe in the Holy Spirit*, I:156.

88   Groppe, "Congar's Theology of the Holy Spirit," 463.

89   Congar, *I Believe in the Holy Spirit*, II:17.

90   Congar, "The Call to Ecumenism," 102.

A LOOK AHEAD

As indicated at the beginning of this chapter, the theologians explored within the different Christian traditions reflect the classical approach, offering insights presumed to be universal in scope, and thus applicable to every person in every time and place without distinction. With the next chapter, however, this text makes a definitive turn to a contextual hermeneutic that focuses on the particularities of individuals and communities and explores the specific ways in which such persons and groups engage the mystery of the Holy Spirit.

This contextual approach began appearing in the 1960s and presented a distinctly different approach to doing theology. This approach contends that every theological statement is "bound to," and shaped by, "a particular historical, socio-cultural, political, and psychological life-situation."[91] Every theological insight, beginning with the scriptures themselves, emerged at a certain place and time for a specific group of people through a particular theologian for an explicit purpose. Every religious activity and experience is influenced and particularized by the personal, social, cultural, and ethnic history, milieu, and worldview of the persons involved. Hence, the task of theology, and in this case pneumatology, has come to be understood as "a dynamic, thoughtful activity that seeks to bring a religious tradition into genuine conversation with some aspect of contemporary experience."[92] Over time, interaction with the social, historical, and cultural particularities of the theologians and their communities have yielded pneumatologies viewed through the human experience of women, African-Americans, Latinx persons, and those who are poor and oppressed throughout the world. It is to pneumatologies rooted in such particularities that this book now turns.

---

91   Emmanuel Clapsis, "The Challenge of Contextual Theologies," *GOTR* 38 (1993): 73.

92   Brennan Hill, Paul Knitter, and William Madges, *Faith, Religion, Theology: A Contemporary Introduction* (Mystic, CT: Twenty-Third Publications, 2002), 287.

FOR REFLECTION

- Have you had the sense of partaking in divinity through the Holy Spirit? How has that realization transformed you?
- How has the Holy Spirit adapted to your capacity to receive the divine self? Was your receptivity expanded, and were you driven beyond yourself in the encounter?
- When has the Spirit inspired a creative mission in you? When, perhaps, a contemplative, obedient receptivity? Compare these experiences.

FOR FURTHER READING

Caponi, Francis J. "Aspects of the Pneumatologies of Karl Rahner and Hans Urs von Balthasar." *New Theology Review* 20:1 (2007): 7–17.

Corcoran, Patrick. "The Holy Spirit and the Life of the Spirit Today." *Proceedings of the Irish Biblical Association* 3 (1979): 97–111.

Groppe, Elizabeth Teresa. "The Contribution of Yves Congar's Theology of the Holy Spirit." *Theological Studies* 62 (2001): 451–78.

Sachs, John R. "*Deus Semper Major—Ad Majorem Dei Gloriam*: The Pneumatology and Spirituality of Hans Urs von Balthasar." *Gregorianum* 74:4 (1993): 631–57.

CHAPTER SIX

The Irruption of the Spirit in Latin America

INTRODUCTION

O F THE CENTRAL ACTIVITIES that can be ascribed to the Holy Spirit, according to theologian Patrick Gardner, one is the ongoing "translation" of the gospel in ways that both enable it to be appropriated by each generation of Christians and that ensure it remains consistent with the teaching of Jesus Christ. Gardner further contends that, in keeping with the Spirit's fidelity to the words and deeds of Jesus, "the process of liberation from social sin or structures of sin is [also] rooted primarily in the mission of the Holy Spirit."[1] Biblical precedents that include Jesus' own claim to fulfilling the prophetic words of Isaiah through the power of the Holy Spirit (Luke 4:18–19), as well as magisterial documents such as *Gaudium et Spes* (§26, 38), *Octogesima Adveniens* (Paul VI), and *Redemptoris Missio* (John Paul II), make evident that the Spirit's power extends beyond liberation from personal sin to the Spirit's liberative action in society. Thus, states Gardner,

> When we Christians encounter the self-liberating and self-humanizing movements of the poor in history, we are forced to acknowledge the Spirit in them, renewing the face of the earth.... So when efforts to overcome these conditions arise—when the poor begin to claim freedom; to have a voice; to form living,

---

[1] Patrick Gardner, "Spirit, Tradition, and the Pneumatology of Liberation," *The Other Journal: An Intersection of Theology & Culture* 23:5 (2014), https://theotherjournal.com/2014/07/14/spirit-tradition-and-the-pneumatology-of-liberation/.

functional communities; and to act in history to alter these structures –…then we are forced to identify God's immanent activity, in some way animating these changes. For the condition of overcoming the power and effects of sin is by definition divine, a condition that only God's direct activity can bring about.[2]

It is this understanding of the person and activity of the Holy Spirit that grounds not only the Latin American pneumatologies examined in this chapter, but also the very hermeneutic of this text as a whole. As Gardner maintains, "If both liberation and Tradition have their common foundation in pneumatology, a concept of Tradition emerges that is fundamentally liberative: one that is only alive…to the extent that it is capable of embodying and fostering the liberation of the oppressed."[3] The Latin American pneumatology explored in this chapter is a primary example of this "fundamentally liberative" nature of the activity of the Holy Spirit. Moreover, it is the first of the *contextual* pneumatologies to be surveyed in forthcoming chapters. Subsequent chapters examine other such contextual pneumatologies of liberation that emerge from communities marginalized because of gender, race, ethnicity, disability, sexual orientation, and environmental despoliation.

Liberation pneumatology, like liberation theology in general, has two principal elements: "First, it stresses liberation from all forms of human oppression: social, economic, political, racial, sexual, environmental, religious, and so on." An additional essential component is "its insistence that theology emerge from the local setting."[4] For the Latin American context in particular, Leonardo Boff writes:

> [The] stage was set for powerful reflection on the Holy Spirit by the irruption of the poor on the political scene; by *aggiornamento* in the Church, which began at Vatican II and was creatively pursued by the bishops at Medellin (1968) and Puebla (1979); and by the renewal of faith through charismatic movements.[5]

---

2   Gardner, "Spirit, Tradition, and the Pneumatology of Liberation."

3   Gardner, "Spirit, Tradition, and the Pneumatology of Liberation."

4   Deane William Ferm, "Third World Liberation Theology: What's It All About?" *Irish Theological Quarterly* 51:4 (1985): 309.

5   Leonardo Boff, *Come, Holy Spirit: Inner Fire, Giver of Life & Comforter of the Poor*, trans. Margaret Wilde (Maryknoll, NY: Orbis, 2015), 109.

This chapter explores the irruption of the Holy Spirit in the context of Latin America through three noted theologians. It opens with the Biblical reflections of Gustavo Gutiérrez in his book *The God of Life*, moves to José Comblin's systematic theology of the Spirit, and concludes with the pneumatology of Leonardo Boff in his book *Come, Holy Spirit: Inner Fire, Giver of Life & Comforter of the Poor*.

LATIN AMERICAN PNEUMATOLOGIES

Gustavo Gutiérrez: "The God Who Liberates Is the God of Life"

At the outset of his book *The God of Life*, Peruvian-born Gustavo Gutiérrez poses the question "How are we to speak of God?" and his answer is "According to the promptings of the Spirit."[6] Despite this apparent reliance on the Holy Spirit to direct his speech about God, Gutiérrez does not have a highly structured pneumatology. Rather, his pneumatology is implicit in many of his writings, especially those works that focus upon spirituality of liberation. Most notable among these writings on spirituality is *We Drink from Our Own Wells: The Spiritual Journey of a People*,[7] which traces the exodus journey of the poor in Latin America with a liberating God toward liberation from poverty, oppression, and death. His reflections on spirituality are an integral part of his groundbreaking efforts to advance a theology of liberation, which earned him the title of "father of liberation theology." This chapter focuses on his examination of the Holy Spirit as presented in *The God of Life*. However, one should not expect an explicit and focused pneumatology from Gutiérrez. Rather, one must glean his understanding of the action of the Holy Spirit through his reflections on the God who liberates in the context of human history. For Gutiérrez, this *Dios liberador* is clearly the Holy Spirit, the God of Life.

---

6   Gustavo Gutiérrez, *The God of Life* (Maryknoll, NY: Orbis, 1991), 1.

7   Gustavo Gutiérrez, *We Drink from Our Own Wells: The Spiritual Journey of a People* (20th anniversary ed.), trans. Matthew J. O'Connell (Maryknoll, NY: Orbis, 2003).

Quoting Black liberation theologian James Cone, who states, "to ask, 'Who is God?' is to focus on what he is doing,"[8] Gutiérrez affirms that this divine doing is "God's liberating action in history."[9] While Gutiérrez deems it correct to understand that God is a liberator, he is quick to focus on the fact that God's historical actions do not make God who God is. Rather, they reveal who God is in God's very nature. Hence, for Gutiérrez, who God is determines what God does in history.

> God is not a liberator because God liberates; rather, God liberates because God is a liberator. God is not just because God establishes justice, or faithful because God enters into a covenant, but the other way around…. God's being gives meaning to God's action.[10]

Gutiérrez indicates that this manifestation of God as liberator stretches from the Exodus experience in the First Testament to the life and mission of Jesus in the Second Testament. The Scriptures reveal a living, holy, and faithful God who liberates people who suffer under the reign of death to the freedom of new and abundant life.

Gutiérrez's correlation of liberation with life is most fully examined in *The God of Life* in his chapter "God Liberates: God Is Life." Focusing first on the Exodus experience of the Jews and then on the messianic proclamation of Jesus of Nazareth, Gutiérrez emphasizes that God's liberating activities flow from the fact that God is a God of life who wills fullness of life for all beings. As he develops this thought, one can see the indissoluble link between God as divine liberator and life-giver with God the Holy Spirit. This is revealed most explicitly in Gutiérrez's reflection on the "programmatic passage" of Luke 4:18–19, in which Jesus proclaims his mission and ministry:

> The Spirit of the Lord is upon me,
> Because he has anointed me
> To bring glad tidings to the poor.
> He has sent me to proclaim liberty to captives and

---

8   James Cone, *A Black Theology of Liberation* (New York: Lippincott, 1970), 142.

9   Gutiérrez, *The God of Life*, 2.

10   Gutiérrez, *The God of Life*, 2.

Recovery of sight to the blind,
To let the oppressed go free,
And to proclaim a year acceptable to the Lord.[11]

According to Gutiérrez, this passage, drawn from the prophet Isaiah
61:1–2, describes the essence of the mission of Jesus of Nazareth, a
mission directly related to the fact that "the Spirit of the Lord" is upon
him. Gutiérrez points out that the human miseries noted in this passage—"poverty, captivity, blindness, and oppression"—are all "manifestations of death."[12] It is "Jesus, who has been anointed Messiah by
the power of the Spirit, [who] will cause death to withdraw, by intro-
ducing a source of life that is meant to bring history to its fulfillment."[13]
Jesus is the servant of Yahweh of whom God says, "Upon him I have put
my spirit; he shall bring forth justice to the nations" (Isaiah 42:1).

Gutiérrez maintains that all the manifestations of death enumer-
ated by Luke are not on the "same level." Following the exegesis of a
similar passage in Matthew's gospel by J. Dupont, Gutiérrez contends
that the most important misery to be addressed and, thus, the primary
purpose of Jesus' ministry in the Spirit, is the proclamation of the good
news to the poor. According to Dupont,

The proclamation of the good news is identical with the cures of the sick;
"proclamation of the good news" is simply a formula that generalizes and
makes explicit the significance of these cures.... In any case, one thing is
certain: the good news proclaimed to the poor can only be the news that
they will cease to be poor and to suffer from poverty. As the blind see and
the deaf hear and the dead come to life, so the poor will not lack what they
need; they will cease to be victims of an unjust distribution of goods.[14]

Gutiérrez considers the release of captives, sight for the blind, and freedom for the oppressed as tangible manifestations of the preeminent

11   Here I am using the translation from *The God of Life*, 6–7.

12   Gutiérrez, *The God of Life*, 7.

13   Gutiérrez, *The God of Life*, 8.

14   J. Dupont, "Jésus annonce la bonne nouvelle aux pauvres," in *Evangelizare pau-
      peribus* (Atti della XXIV Settimana Biblica) (Brescia: Paideia, 1978), 183.

preaching of good news to the poor who lack the basic necessities of life, a preaching that may be summarized as a declaration of freedom,[15] which "the Bible connects…with the presence of the Spirit."[16]

Gutiérrez notes that the writer of Luke's gospel appropriates not only portions of the passage of Isaiah 61, but also adds the phrase "to let the oppressed go free" found in Isaiah 58:6:

> Is this not, rather, the fast that I choose:
> releasing those bound unjustly,
> untying the thongs of the yoke;
> Setting free the oppressed,
> breaking off every yoke?

This is further evidence for Gutiérrez that the effect of the Spirit's anointing is focused on the liberation of the poor. This is borne out in Isaiah's reference to "a year acceptable to the Lord," which refers to the Jewish jubilee year, an event that "clearly had to do with liberation."[17] As Leviticus 25:10 proclaims, "This fiftieth year you shall make sacred by proclaiming liberty in the land for all its inhabitants." The aim of the jubilee year was to rectify inequalities and injustice, to forgive debts, to return property, to free slaves, and to let the land lie fallow, all in recognition of the sovereignty of God over the land and people of Israel. It was meant to restore right relationship among all inhabitants and ultimately with the God of life.

Hence, Gutiérrez insists that the liberation proclaimed by the Spirit-filled Jesus did not point to a future time of deliverance and fulfillment. Like the jubilee year, the reign of God is meant to be a historical reality, "the ultimate meaning of history."[18] As Jesus states in Luke 4:21, "*Today* this Scripture passage is fulfilled in your hearing." Thus, the liberation prompted by the Holy Spirit, the *Dios liberador*, lives in the midst of God's people in the person of Jesus and in all those who walk according to the Spirit in discipleship. Through the inspiration

---

15   Gutiérrez, *The God of Life*, 8.

16   Gutiérrez, *The God of Life*, 142.

17   Gutiérrez, *The God of Life*, 9.

18   Gutiérrez, *The God of Life*, 9.

of the Spirit, "God is present wherever the gift of the kingdom and its demands are welcomed into our lives and activities."[19]

As the event of Pentecost manifested the power of the Holy Spirit, God as Spirit continuously empowers persons to announce the God of life even in the midst of death and injustice. Nonetheless, liberation consistent with the reign of God is not guaranteed. Even after Jesus' proclamation of his Spirit-filled mission through the words of the prophet Isaiah, those who heard him wanted to kill him and silence his message (Luke 4:28–30). Even today, rejection meets those who proclaim liberation for the oppressed and marginalized in Latin American society and church and throughout the world. However, Gutiérrez asserts, those who walk in the Spirit are continuously impelled to announce the reign of God through "actions that bear witness to the resurrection of the Lord, and [through] words that proclaim life to be the ultimate meaning of human history."[20]

José Comblin: "The Spirit as Liberating Life and Action"[21]

According to theologian Leonardo Boff, the most outstanding theologian in the area of Latin American pneumatology is José Comblin, who spent more than twenty-five years exploring the Holy Spirit, "trying to understand what it is doing on Earth, and where it is working."[22] Comblin was a Belgian-born theologian who lived in both Chile and Brazil. In his essay on the Holy Spirit, published in *Mysterium Liberationis: Fundamental Concepts of Liberation Theology*, he echoed Boff's contention about the significance of the episcopal conferences of Medellín and Puebla concerning the activity of the Spirit in the irruption of the poor in Latin America. Quoting from the final document of the Puebla Conference, Comblin asserted:

> The renovation of human beings, and subsequently of society, will depend first of all on the action of the Holy Spirit...[who] continues to arouse

---

19   Gutiérrez, *The God of Life*, 141.

20   Gutiérrez, *The God of Life*, 144.

21   From Boff, *Come, Holy Spirit*, 109.

22   José Comblin, *A vida: em busca da libertad*, 8, in Boff, *Come, Holy Spirit*, 109.

yearning for liberative salvation in our peoples. Hence, we must discover
the Spirit's authentic presence in the history of Latin America.[23]

Despite the emphasis on the action of the Holy Spirit by both of
these conferences, neither they nor Latin American theology in general has constructed an explicit pneumatology. This may be, according to Comblin, because the experience of the Holy Spirit is often
anonymous.[24]

According to Comblin, while both Christian and Jewish persons
are acquainted with the notion of the *Dios liberador*, the God who delivers, few identify this with the Holy Spirit. Unlike the Exodus, God no
longer delivers people through force or miracles. Rather, *Dios liberador*
works through "the forces and energies that God places within people," by enlightenment, charism, solidarity, and enthusiasm—in their
midst and through their actions.[25] Moreover, when Christians inter-
pret their liberative impulses and actions in the light of the Scriptures,
they recognize the *Dios liberador* as the Holy Spirit as Jesus himself did:

> The Spirit of the Lord is upon me;
> therefore, he has anointed me.
> He has sent me to bring glad tidings to the poor,
> to proclaim liberty to captives,
> Recovery of sight to the blind,
> and release to prisoners,
> To announce a year of favor from the Lord.
> (Luke 4:18–19)

Comblin acknowledged that there has not been sufficient stress on the
relationship between liberation and the Holy Spirit, despite the fact
that the Gospels and Epistles draw such conclusions. Comblin pointed
out that this may be due to the fact that "a theology of the Holy Spirit

---

23   José Comblin, "The Holy Spirit," in *Mysterium Liberationis: Fundamental
     Concepts of Liberation Theology*, ed. Ignacio Ellacuría, SJ, and Jon Sobrino, SJ
     (Maryknoll, NY: Orbis, 1993), 462.

24   Comblin, "The Holy Spirit," 463.

25   Comblin, "The Holy Spirit," 464.

can emerge only from the praxis of a free Christian people."[26] The first expression of this praxis of freedom, Comblin maintained, is *the word*.

> A word of this kind denounces the silence in which the peoples have been kept under the thumb of the oppressor.... It announces a new life, a different society. It calls together and unites the poor. It stimulates, it animates.... The Holy Spirit is at the root of the cry of the Christian people groaning in the hope of resurrection.[27]

A second expression of the Spirit's liberating activity is the emergence of *Christian community* with "a force at work within them that arouses generosity, dedication, and sacrifice."[28] Comblin likened it to the sense of renewal in the early age of the Church, when communities reached out beyond themselves in kinship rather than oppression. The primary sign of these communities is charity which, as Paul wrote, is the greatest of the Spirit's charisms, creating "humanity-in-communion...a promise of renewal for all society."[29] This leads to a final manifestation of the Holy Spirit in Comblin's schema—*life* in the midst of death. Comblin declared that the Biblical God is a God of life and that this God of life is the Holy Spirit. Citing the prophet Ezekiel and the apostle Paul, Comblin held that the Spirit has been associated with new life in both Testaments, especially manifested in the resurrection of Jesus the Christ from the dead. In a people broken by poverty, oppression, and death, the Spirit gives a new vitality and a hope of liberation; as the creed proclaims, the Holy Spirit is truly "the giver of life."

It is obvious in Comblin's pneumatology that the Holy Spirit cannot be reduced to an experience of interiority. Rather, the Spirit is cosmic in dimension. It is the same Spirit who swept over the primordial waters, who vivifies all created beings, who fills and renews the face of the earth. Moreover, like Yahweh, who chose Israel, the least of all peoples (Deuteronomy 7:7), the Holy Spirit "acts in the world by means of

---

26   Comblin, "The Holy Spirit," 467.

27   Comblin, "The Holy Spirit," 468.

28   Comblin, "The Holy Spirit," 470.

29   Comblin, "The Holy Spirit," 470.

the poor."[30] Operating on "the underside of history," the Spirit counteracts violence and exploitation through "patience, perseverance,
protest, petition."[31] From such interaction with the poor of the earth,
the church itself is born—not of the center, but of the periphery. In the
Spirit, "the church celebrates the event of liberation."[32]

This leads Comblin to propose a spirituality of liberation that
"springs from the simultaneous practice of thousands of committed
Christians" in similar concrete conditions.[33] According to Comblin,
this spirituality is one of "integral liberation," through the activity of
the Holy Spirit, who frees them from injustice, oppression, and all
forms of slavery. Not found in books, but in the personal experience of
the poor, such liberation "engenders no pride, selfishness, [or] indi-
vidualism," but rather inspires service and solidarity in community.
"The basic theme of this spirituality," Comblin concluded, "is the old-
est Christian theme of all."

> It is the theme of the gospels themselves: the following of Jesus in his
> humanity—the imitation of the works of Jesus over the course of his earthly
> mission.... The Spirit shows them the hidden correspondences. And, lo,
> the life of Jesus revives, in the hidden, heroic life of the church of the poor.[34]

Leonardo Boff: "The Pneumatization of the Feminine"

"We live in dangerous times," claims Leonardo Boff, "which call us to
serious reflection on the *Spiritus Creator.*"[35] However, to do so requires
a paradigm beyond traditional Western theological discourse.

---

30   Comblin, "The Holy Spirit," 474.

31   Comblin, "The Holy Spirit," 474.

32   Comblin, "The Holy Spirit," 479.

33   Comblin, "The Holy Spirit," 481.

34   Comblin, "The Holy Spirit," 482.

35   Boff, *Come, Holy Spirit*, vii.

To think of the Spirit is to think of movement, action, process, appearance, story, and the irruption of something new and surprising. It means thinking about what we are constantly becoming. These are not things that can be described in classical concepts.... [We] need a different paradigm... [that] helps us see the genesis of all things: their emergence out of the Unnamable, Mysterious, Loving Energy that...penetrates creation from beginning to end.[36]

Before exploring this new paradigm in his book *Come, Holy Spirit: Inner Fire, Giver of Life & Comforter of the Poor*, Boff offers an examination of the classical language and paradigms, both Eastern and Western, that heretofore have been used to speak of the Holy Spirit, especially in relation to the Trinity as a whole. His search for new images and models takes him in the direction of the feminine[37] and the universe.

Calling his venture the "pneumatization of the feminine," Boff commences this exploration by noting that the self-revelation of the Divine is customarily viewed from a top-down perspective. God communicates the Divine self to the human person and to the universe unconditionally and draws them in to become one with God. However, he proposes that one can also view this dynamic from the bottom up: "From the heart of the evolutionary process, always sustained and inhabited by the Trinity, the divine Persons well up in those bearers who have been prepared by the universe and by God's action to take one of the divine Persons into themselves."[38]

Boff's expansion of this insight focuses on the indwelling of the Holy Spirit in Mary of Nazareth. In Boff's words, "The Spirit stepped out of its transcendence and took Mary into itself so radically that she was spiritualized...or pneumatized."[39] The Spirit did so, according to Boff, in such a way that Mary now belonged to the Holy Spirit,

---

36 Boff, *Come, Holy Spirit*, viii.

37 Most feminist theologians would contest Boff's use of the term *feminine*, since it represents a culturally derived construct and stereotype that has contributed to the very oppression and marginalization of women that he is trying to counteract with this construct.

38 Boff, *Come, Holy Spirit*, 118.

39 Boff, *Come, Holy Spirit*, 118.

who formed with her a single reality without obscuring the distinction between Creator and creature. There are obvious parallels between this action of the Spirit in Mary and that of the self-communication of the Word in Jesus of Nazareth, "which led to the incarnation of the Son or the divinization of the man."[40] Boff, however, does not use the term *incarnation* when describing the instantiation of the Holy Spirit within Mary, preferring instead *pneumatization*.

To buttress his proposal concerning "this culminating event in the history of the universe and humanity," Boff cites Luke 1:35, which tells of the overshadowing of Mary by the Holy Spirit. He points out that the first divine Person to "break into" the universe was not the Son, but the Holy Spirit. "The third Person in the order of the Trinity comes first in the order of creation,"[41] which represents a clear challenge to the predominant christomonism of Christianity and theology.

Boff provides three indicators to support his proposal of the pneumatization of Mary. First, he specifies the similarity of terminology between the prologue of John (1:14) and the annunciation to Mary. In both cases, the term used is *episkiásei*, Greek for "pitch its tent." This signifies a permanent indwelling in Mary by the Holy Spirit, not a temporary prophetic mission. Second, it is Mary's unconditional assent to this indwelling of the Spirit that enables the subsequent incarnation of the Son. Finally, the order of events as told in Luke 1:35 presents a clear logic: "*Therefore* the child to be born will be…called Son of God." This sequence clearly indicates that "the Holy Spirit is taken into her person; she is raised to the level of God the Spirit; only God can beget the Son of God. Only Mary, taken into and identified with God the Holy Spirit, can bear a Holy One, a Son of God."[42]

Despite the clarity with which he lays out his understanding of the pneumatization of Mary by the Holy Spirit based on this Lukan passage, Boff notes that centuries of theologians have virtually ignored the significance of this passage when formulating their pneumatologies.[43]

---

40   Boff, *Come, Holy Spirit*, 118.

41   Boff, *Come, Holy Spirit*, 119.

42   Boff, *Come, Holy Spirit*, 119.

43   Boff lists Jürgen Moltmann, Michael Welker, Heribert Mühlen, Yves Congar, and José Comblin among those noted theologians of the Holy Spirit who do not

Boff sees in this the "masculinizing, patriarchal" blindness of theology and of the Christian ecclesial tradition. He calls for "a self-critical awareness of our social location and of the ways our masculinity conditions all our theological reflection"—a tendency, Boff asserts, that is evident among noted women theologians whom he indicts as becoming dependent on the theology of men.[44] This dependence constrains "the struggle for the full liberation of women in society." According to Boff, women theologians have "become hostages to the Christology of the Son of God made man and failed to grasp the divine element in their reality as women."

> They have not discovered, or known how to express, the relationship of the Holy Spirit to women's life and the role of Mary in the mystery of salvation, which shows us the face of God the Mother, of infinite tenderness and compassion.[45]

Boff points out instances in the First Testament[46] of the Spirit's association with women and their activities, particularly in the feminine gendered nouns *ruah* and *shekinah* (Hebrew) and in the personification of Wisdom as female. The Second Testament also highlights the centrality of Mary, whose response to God's call and acceptance of the Spirit empowered the incarnation. She is the Spirit-bearer in whom is the Holy Spirit, "the personification of love at its most selfless, most generous, most self-giving, like the love of a mother."[47]

"present her as the one who reveals the feminine, maternal face of God." Boff, *Come, Holy Spirit*, 120.

44 Boff, *Come, Holy Spirit*, 121.

45 Boff, *Come, Holy Spirit*, 121.

46 This usage refers to what is customarily called the Old Testament, as the Second Testament refers to the New Testament.

47 Boff, *Come, Holy Spirit*, 122. Boff associates the Spirit's activities with actions that he states are "primarily (but not exclusively) considered feminine, relating to motherhood," such as caring, helping, inspiring, protecting, accepting, forgiving, and comforting. Many feminist theologians would critique Boff's descriptors as gender-stereotypical, which does not, in fact, advance the liberation of women.

Removing patriarchal blinders not only in theology, but also to the pneumatization of Mary, Boff asserts, is critical for the human community, female and male alike. In the pneumatization of Mary, something in humanity itself has become divine, has entered the divine presence, "has become eternal."[48] While uplifting for female and male alike, this realization is particularly liberating for women, Boff argues, who have been prepared for millennia for this arrival of the Spirit within them. In the pneumatization of Mary by the Holy Spirit, all women are pneumatized and, in the fullness of time, "women and the whole universe will achieve fulfillment and convergence."

> Then the Kingdom of the Trinity, Father, Son, and Holy Spirit, will break through from outside and inside. From the beginning the Spirit has been working quietly within the process of evolution, to bring it to full fruition.[49]

A LOOK AHEAD

To some extent, the pneumatology of Boff, with its pneumatization of Mary and its liberation of women, prepares the way for the next chapter's exploration of feminist pneumatology through the contributions of women from different cultural contexts. Belying Boff's contention that women theologians are impeded by their failure "to grasp the divine element in their reality as women," the feminist pneumatologies that are presented appropriate a diverse range of female imagery and actions to speak of the Holy Spirit present and dynamic in and through the lives of women. The fact that the women theologians presented here do not employ the person and model of Mary of Nazareth to structure their pneumatologies does not signal their failure to jettison the constraints of patriarchal theology. Rather, they seek to explore and address the Holy Spirit on her own terms and in her divine personhood to assert her significance to women's lives and liberation.

---

48   Boff, *Come, Holy Spirit*, 123. Boff seems to discount the full humanity of Jesus in these statements. Nonetheless, his emphasis here is clearly on the Holy Spirit within Mary, which he sees as a lacuna in theology.

49   Boff, *Come, Holy Spirit*, 124.

FOR REFLECTION

- The passage from Luke 4:18–19 is critical for liberation pneumatology. Reflect on that passage. How did the Spirit's anointing shape Jesus' ministry? To what does the Spirit call you?
- Has *Dios liberador* worked in your life through "the forces and energies" that the Spirit placed within you?
- What is your response to Boff's proposal about the Spirit's *pneumatization* of Mary? Have you ever experienced belonging to the Spirit? What new life did that birth on you?

FOR FURTHER READING

Boff, Leonardo. *Come, Holy Spirit: Inner Fire, Giver of Life & Comforter of the Poor*, trans. Margaret Wilde. Maryknoll, NY: Orbis, 2015.

Ferm, Deane William. "Third World Liberation Theology: What's It All About?" *Irish Theological Quarterly* 51:4 (1985): 309–18.

Gardner, Patrick. "Spirit, Tradition, and the Pneumatology of Liberation." *The Other Journal: An Intersection of Theology & Culture* 23:5 (2014), https://theotherjournal.com/2014/07/14/spirit-tradition-and-the-pneumatology-of-liberation/.

Gutiérrez, Gustavo. *The God of Life*. Maryknoll, NY: Orbis, 1991.

CHAPTER SEVEN

Out of the Silence

The Holy Spirit in Feminist Discourse

INTRODUCTION

IN HER INCISIVE ESSAY on feminist pneumatology, theologian Helen Bergin argues for the significance of attention to the topic "because it brings together two voices often rendered silent in mainstream theology, namely the Spirit of God and women."[1] Bergin lays out five "initial concerns" that feminist theologians encounter in formulating a feminist pneumatology. The first involves the positioning of the Holy Spirit as the third divine person within the Trinity, which can imply that the Spirit is somehow "derivative" from the Father and the Son rather than unique in her own right.[2] A related matter is the long-standing identification of the Spirit as the communion between, the shared love of, or the gift given by the Father and the Son. Bergin notes that this may imply that the Spirit is not only "sandwiched between" the two more distinctive persons, but also suggests a certain passivity of the third person.

---

1   Helen Bergin, "Feminist Pneumatology," *Colloquium* 42:2 (2010): 188.

2   Throughout this chapter, I will follow the recent feminist convention of using the female pronoun when referring to the Holy Spirit. Nonetheless, Bergin says, there is an inherent danger even here. "The Spirit who has the above-mentioned qualities of 'coming last' in Trinitarian blessings, or being held between Father and Son, finds herself in a more dangerous position than ever. The female third person falls back into her customary place." Bergin, "Feminist Pneumatology," 191.

The third concern that Bergin points to is a perhaps unrecognized limitation inherent in the naming of the Father and the Son. Each naming fails to indicate that, as God, both Father and Son are also Spirit (John 4:24). As a result, the Holy Spirit seems to lack an identity and particularity of her own. Bergin then moves from the intradivine life to the life of the Spirit in history. Indicating that the Spirit is often characterized as dwelling within the human person, Bergin is concerned that such a focus restricts and privatizes "what is a boundless and infinite divine gift with social and cosmic dimensions." This leads to Bergin's final critique that much speech concerning the Spirit is anthropocentric, and thus limits the Spirit's reach to the human, rather than to all creation.[3] Therefore, in their quest to develop feminist pneumatologies, theologians must approach theological texts and sources with a hermeneutics of suspicion toward androcentric thinking, with attention to women's missing or misrepresented voices, and with a praxis for transformation and the making of justice.[4]

The theologians in this chapter clearly model these principles in their pneumatologies from a feminist perspective. In "The Holy Spirit and Gender Equality: A Latin American Perspective," Patricia Urueña Barbosa proposes to "reinterpret the Spirit's presence and action from a liberating perspective" in order to promote more equal social structures, justice, and peace.[5] Using womanist theological anthropology in her essay "The Holy Spirit and Black Women: A Womanist Perspective," Linda Thomas contends that the "historical radical marginality" of Black women centers them in realities in which "unconventional wisdom dwells."[6] Finally, attending to women's missing experiences or misrepresented voices, Elizabeth Johnson in *She Who Is: The Mystery of God in Feminist Theological Discourse* speaks about God

---

3   Bergin, "Feminist Pneumatology," 189–90.

4   Bergin, "Feminist Pneumatology," 191–92.

5   Patricia Urueña Barbosa, "The Holy Spirit and Gender Equality: A Latin American Perspective," *Vision* 13:1 (Spring 2012): 40–47.

6   Linda Thomas, "The Holy Spirit and Black Women," in *Christian Doctrines for Global Gender Justice*, ed. Jenny Daggers and Grace Ji-Sun Kim (New York: Palgrave Macmillan, 2015), 73.

"from the world's history"[7] and advances a pneumatology of Spirit-Sophia, the "divinity drawing near and passing by" all of creation.[8]

THE HOLY SPIRIT IN FEMINIST DISCOURSE

Patricia Urueña Barbosa: "Spirit-Wisdom"

"To see the Holy Spirit from the perspective of churches that work for peace and justice," contends Patricia Urueña Barbosa, "is to understand the liberating, empowering, and transformative dynamic of the work of God's Spirit among us."[9] This perspective moves Urueña Barbosa, a Mennonite Mission Network worker in Ecuador, to assert that churches cannot authentically work for peace and justice in the world if they do not first examine "the relationships of domination and exclusion" within their own traditions and communities of faith. The approach that Urueña Barbosa takes is a theological one, examining the patriarchal beliefs that have led to the marginalization of women in church and society. She calls for revision of those traditions that uphold the superiority of men and inferiority of women, as well as the teaching that lays the responsibility for the fall, for sin, and for evil on the shoulders of women. Such traditions, Urueña Barbosa maintains, are responsible not only for the asymmetrical relationships between male and female, but also "unjust...economic structures...and evils such as xenophobia, racism, domination, colonization, wars, exploitation of natural resources, destruction of the environment, and death."[10] She proposes the need for a theology that establishes equal and supportive relationships among peoples, with God, and for creation. To do so, Urueña Barbosa focuses upon the presence and action of the Spirit of God in the world. Like others before her, she notes the inattention of theology toward pneumatology in its constructive efforts. "The Spirit

---

7   Elizabeth A. Johnson, *She Who Is: The Mystery of God in Feminist Theological Discourse* (New York: Crossroad, 1992).

8   Johnson, *She Who Is*, 124.

9   Urueña Barbosa, "The Holy Spirit and Gender Equality," 40.

10 Urueña Barbosa, "The Holy Spirit and Gender Equality," 40–41.

has been forgotten and marginalized by theologies, both traditional and contemporary," relegated like Cinderella to being "the neglected stepsister...largely unrecognized, lost in obscurity."[11]

Carrying the metaphor forward, Urueña Barbosa envisions the marginalized women of Latin America as Cinderellas in their own right, oppressed and mistreated with their gifts unrecognized.[12] Many women continue to live in patriarchal contexts of "social injustice and religious exclusion" that limit their full participation in church and society. According to Urueña Barbosa,

> These constraints limit their possibilities for self-improvement and inde-
> pendence.... A setting in which these attitudes prevail becomes a breeding
> ground for male domination of women, for violence and abuse that women
> suffer at the hands of men. These multiple forms of marginalization and
> death are the experience not only of Latin American women but of women
> throughout the world where structures of domination and exclusion con-
> tinue to determine their lives.[13]

This moves Urueña Barbosa to consider the relationship between such patriarchal marginalization and neglect and the obscurity of the Holy Spirit in theological study.

Urueña Barbosa proposes to reinterpret the Holy Spirit from a liberative perspective, envisioning the Spirit of a God who "does not marginalize, oppress, or exercise control over or use violence against," and who promotes "fulfillment in a life of justice and peace."[14] The result, she contends, is a world in which just and equal social structures can emerge, while colonialism, exclusion, and violence cease. Urueña Barbosa is clear that her goal is to "overcome the dualisms of gender that perpetuate injustice."[15] As a result, she does not pursue a path that attributes socially constructed feminine characteristics on

---

11   Urueña Barbosa, "The Holy Spirit and Gender Equality," 41.

12   Urueña Barbosa, "The Holy Spirit and Gender Equality," 42.

13   Urueña Barbosa, "The Holy Spirit and Gender Equality," 42.

14   Urueña Barbosa, "The Holy Spirit and Gender Equality," 43.

15   Urueña Barbosa, "The Holy Spirit and Gender Equality," 43.

an otherwise masculine image of God, but rather strives to "discover a God in whose image we—women and men—were created, a God with whom all human beings can identify...[who] is our strength and hope in this world of injustice, pain, and death."[16]

Urueña Barbosa roots her constructive enterprise in the Hebrew Scriptures, and more specifically in the Wisdom books of Proverbs 1–9, Sirach, and the Wisdom of Solomon. She notes that in each of these texts the terms related to the Spirit are grammatically feminine—*shekinah* (the presence of God), *ruah* (the breath of God), and *hokmah* (the wisdom of God). *Shekinah* connotes the permanence of God's presence among the people of Israel, *ruah* points to the creative power of God from the beginning of the world, and *hokmah* is the personification of the Divine Presence in the Wisdom Literature. The last of these, *hokmah*, is more often denominated in the literature by the Greek female term *Sophia*, the Spirit as Wisdom, and provides a robust symbol for the Divine as the giver of life. Her constructive work advances three female images of Spirit-Wisdom: as giver of life, as maternal face of God, and as proclaimer of justice.

SPIRIT-WISDOM—GIVER OF LIFE

The book of Proverbs proclaims that Wisdom was with God before the creation of the world, present as the creative, generative, and ordering principle of life (Proverbs 8). In Sirach 24, Spirit-Wisdom describes her own activities:

> I came forth from the mouth of the Most High and covered the earth like a mist.
>   I dwelt in the highest heavens, and my throne was in a pillar of cloud.
> Alone I compassed the vault of heaven and traversed the depths of the abyss.
> Over waves of the sea, over all the earth, and over every people and nation I
>   have held sway.
> Among all these I sought a resting place; in whose territory should I abide?
>   (24:3–7)

In these verses, Urueña Barbosa sees an ecological perspective as well as mandate. As Spirit-Wisdom sustains creation, she calls her

---

16 Urueña Barbosa, "The Holy Spirit and Gender Equality," 43.

daughter and sons to "have solidarity with and responsibility for tak-
ing care of the biosphere to sustain life."[17]

SPIRIT-WISDOM—MATERNAL FACE OF GOD

Urueña Barbosa moves to the book of the prophet Isaiah to demonstrate the maternal power of the Divine Spirit. The prophet describes
the Divine as the one who carries Israel in her womb and bears them
into old age:

> Listen to me, O house of Jacob, all the remnant of the house of Israel,
> who have been borne by me from your birth, carried from the womb;
> even to your old age…, even when you turn gray I will carry you.
> I have made, and I will bear; I will carry and will save.
>
> (46:3–4)

Her nurturance is demonstrated by the prophet Hosea, who described
the Divine as holding Israel to her cheek (11:4), teaching Ephraim to
walk (11:3), and bending down to feed her children (11:4). While some
mothers may forget their children, the prophet Isaiah assures Israel
that Spirit-Wisdom will never forget her child or fail to show compassion for the child of her womb: "Even these may forget, yet I will
not forget you. See, I have inscribed you on the palms of my hands"
(49:15–16). In these images, Urueña Barbosa finds a strong maternal
face of the Spirit, which is not, however, limited to nurturance, but
also includes bringing justice and righteousness to the peoples (Isaiah
42:1–4). Here Urueña Barbosa sees an integration of nurturance and
governance generally relegated separately to females and males, and,
thus, an overthrow of patriarchal stereotypes.[18]

SPIRIT-WISDOM: PROCLAIMER OF JUSTICE

Finally, through the book of Proverbs, Urueña Barbosa envisions
Spirit-Wisdom as "a cosmic figure who administers justice, is the

---

17   Urueña Barbosa, "The Holy Spirit and Gender Equality," 45.

18   Urueña Barbosa, "The Holy Spirit and Gender Equality," 45.

embodiment of God, and is God."[19] In these chapters, Spirit-Wisdom reaches beyond an attribute of the Divine to full personification as she raises her voice in the streets and calls people to follow her ways:

> Does not Wisdom call, and does not understanding raise her voice?
> On the heights, beside the way, at the crossroads she takes her stand;
> beside the gates in front of the town, at the entrance of the portals she cries out:
> "To you, O people, I call, and my cry is to all that live.
> O simple ones, learn prudence; acquire intelligence, you who lack it.
> Hear, for I will speak noble things, and from my lips will come what is right....
> By me kings reign, and rulers decree what is just;
> by me rulers rule, and nobles, all who govern rightly."
> (Proverbs 8:1–6, 15–16)

Urueña Barbosa specifically notes how Spirit-Wisdom manifests herself in the streets where not only are there people who engage in business and economic activities, but also those who are homeless, dehumanized, and marginalized. She invites the outcast in particular to dine at her table, to "Come, eat of my bread and drink of the wine I have mixed" (Proverbs 9:5). Spirit-Wisdom "leads humanity to great things, inspiring and bringing wisdom. Through her guidance, people find life."[20]

Ultimately, for Urueña Barbosa, "the call of Spirit-Wisdom is an inclusive call,"[21] not simply for women but for all humanity. The holy Spirit as Wisdom is the symbol of justice and equitable relationships within multiple spheres—"personal, ecclesiastic, economic, politic, cultural, and social spheres, and with creation."[22] Abandoning the image of the patriarchal God, which Urueña Barbosa asserts "creates hierarchies; and that excludes, oppresses, and exploits nature," and embracing the image of Spirit-Wisdom "gives us resources for overcoming the marginalization, abuse, and oppression of human Cinderellas, and for opening possibilities for women to experience the

---

19 Urueña Barbosa, "The Holy Spirit and Gender Equality," 45.

20 Urueña Barbosa, "The Holy Spirit and Gender Equality," 46.

21 Urueña Barbosa, "The Holy Spirit and Gender Equality," 46.

22 Urueña Barbosa, "The Holy Spirit and Gender Equality," 46.

fullness of life."[23] Such reinterpretation enables women to envision themselves as created in God's image with the freedom and equality that portends. Because of this, "Spirit-Wisdom is a symbol of hope," fostering inclusive communities of peers, just societies, and equitable distribution of resources, "celebrating what God has given to all humanity for the sustenance of life."[24]

Linda E. Thomas: "The Memory of the Future"

Writing from the perspective of womanist anthropology, theologian Linda E. Thomas discusses "the work of the Holy Spirit in the struggles of black women for liberation and flourishing of life."[25] Bringing African cosmology to bear on Christian tradition in dialogue with Black women's experiences of both brutalization and strength, Thomas demonstrates how Christian ideas concerning the Spirit are "expanded, enriched, and significantly modified by and through how they are uniquely appropriated by black women."[26] In so doing, Black women produced a unique religious perspective on the Holy Spirit that brings distinctive features to the Christian pneumatological framework.

The principal framework that surrounds and supports womanist notions of the Holy Spirit is Black women's lived experience of suffering and struggle, rooted in slavery and persisting to this day in systemic racism and its deleterious effects. Nonetheless, the Spirit is present in this suffering, according to Thomas, moving Black women forward toward freedom and liberation as they resist subjugation. To demonstrate this dynamic, Thomas traces the myriad realities of marginality suffered by Black women since 1619, when African women and men were "stolen away from the continent [and] entered a world vastly different from their homeland" in Jamestown, Virginia.

> [The] majority would be treated as cargo and property, thought to be less than human, and brutally mistreated. The system of white supremacy and

23   Urueña Barbosa, "The Holy Spirit and Gender Equality," 46.

24   Urueña Barbosa, "The Holy Spirit and Gender Equality," 47.

25   Thomas, "The Holy Spirit and Black Women," 73.

26   Thomas, "The Holy Spirit and Black Women," 73.

male superiority would dominate their lives from 1619 forward. Black
women's everyday lives necessitated that they live in two different worlds
at the same time: "one White privileged and oppressive, the other Black,
exploited, and oppressed."[27]

In this captivity, where white slaveowners controlled Black women
and their children, Black women's sexuality was viewed as a com-
modity; women were expected to furnish offspring for the plantation
system. This not only atrociously impacted the Black woman herself,
but also robbed her of stable family relationships, since husbands
and children could be snatched away and marketed as slaves at any
time. Black women continued to fare dreadfully post-slavery through
Reconstruction and the Great Migration north; those who were
employed had demeaning jobs, were poorly paid, and had little time
to spend with family or children. To this day, as Katie Cannon points
out, "Black women are still the victims of the aggravated inequities and
the tridimensional phenomenon of race/class/gender oppression."[28]

Nonetheless, according to Thomas, the insight that Black women
have into the Spirit arises even within these myriad experiences of
suffering, indignity, and oppression.

> On the one hand, insight into the Spirit comes through the enduring ways
> that black women have called on Jesus and the Holy Spirit to be ever present
> in their lives. On the other hand, insight comes from African understand-
> ings of the Spirit as God present in creation, giving and nourishing all life.[29]

Recognizing the Spirit present in their struggles, Black women turn
to the Scriptures to inform their sense of the Holy Spirit. Biblical passages assure Black women "that God's Spirit rekindled dry bones into
a living body (Ezekiel 37),"

---

27   Thomas, "The Holy Spirit and Black Women," 75; interior quote, Katie Cannon,
     "The Emergence of Black Feminist Consciousness," in *Katie Cannon: Womanism
     and the Soul of the Black Community* (New York: Continuum, 2003), 47.

28   Cannon, "The Emergence of Black Feminist Consciousness," 56.

29   Thomas, "The Holy Spirit and Black Women," 74.

...that God's Spirit descended when Jesus was baptized by John the Baptist (Matthew 3:16; Mark 1:10; Luke 3:22); that Jesus declares the Spirit was upon him (Luke 4:16–18); that Jesus promises the disciples that the Holy Spirit will come (John 14:15–25); that Jesus tells them that the Spirit will give them power (Acts 1:8); and that at Pentecost, the Spirit came and the church was birthed (Acts 2).[30]

Furthermore, their African spirituality reminds Black women that all creation reveals the Divine, and thus there is no separation between the sacred and the secular. As a result, Thomas concludes, Black women inherit their wisdom concerning the Spirit through resources both Christian and African, as "the fulfillment of grace, and the active presence of God in their lives as they seek justice from structurally harmful systems."[31] In this weaving, African cosmology contributes a link between freedom, justice, well-being, good health, and flourishing as basic goals in life. "Elaborate cosmologies" of divinities and ancestors paved the way to an understanding of the Holy Spirit, the God who was "inside everything and transcended everything."[32]

This intermingling of African and Christian traditions influenced womanist pneumatology, as it stressed "both the oneness of the Spirit and its simultaneous multivocality, which is the gift of Pentecost—hearing/experiencing/feeling/inheriting one Spirit in languages that correspond with the hearers."[33] It enabled Black women to survive and navigate the unjust suffering they endured in their lives and to embrace the Scriptures that proclaim the impact of the Spirit on liberation and justice. Key to this, according to Thomas, is the proclamation in Isaiah:

Here is my servant, whom I uphold, my chosen, in whom my soul delights;
I have put my spirit upon him; he will bring forth justice to the nations.
He will not cry or lift up his voice, or make it heard in the street;
a bruised reed he will not break, and a dimly burning wick he will not quench;

---

30   Thomas, "The Holy Spirit and Black Women," 74.

31   Thomas, "The Holy Spirit and Black Women," 74.

32   Rebecca K. Harrison, in Thomas, "The Holy Spirit and Black Women," 78.

33   Eboni Marshall Turman, in Thomas, "The Holy Spirit and Black Women," 78.

he will faithfully bring forth justice.

He will not grow faint or be crushed until he has established justice in the earth;

and the coastlands wait for his teaching. (42:1–4)

While the servant knows that the mission is to bring justice, the servant is equally clear that, like Black women throughout history, this will be accomplished in the midst of struggle and bouts of hopelessness (Isaiah 49:4),[34] as well as brutality and suffering (Isaiah 50:6).[35] And yet, as the Holy Spirit sustained the servant in that mission of liberation, the same Spirit upholds Black women in their struggle for justice and to establish the reign of God. "The creative power of the Spirit…makes people aware of their own dignity, of the contradiction between what is and what might be, and that enables them to hold those two together in a single empowering vision."[36] The Spirit empowers Black women to have a "memory of the future,"[37] the knowledge of their present suffering in the context of the reign of God to come. Proclaiming "no" to the destructive powers of racism, poverty, and injustice, and "yes" to the Holy Spirit that sustains and transforms their lives enables Black women to "struggle until we have changed the present reality into the just and free and loving community that we envision"[38] in the coming reign of God.

Elizabeth A. Johnson: "Spirit-Sophia"

In her celebrated work *She Who Is: The Mystery of God in Feminist Theological Discourse*, Elizabeth Johnson tells the story of her struggle

---

34   Isaiah 49:4: "I have labored in vain, I have spent my strength for nothing."

35   Isaiah 50:6: "I gave my back to those who struck me…I did not hide my face from insult and spitting."

36   John P. Brown, "The Holy Spirit in the Struggles of People for Liberation and Fullness of Life," *International Review of Mission* 79:315 (1990): 274.

37   Brown, "The Holy Spirit in the Struggles of People for Liberation and Fullness of Life," 274.

38   Brown, "The Holy Spirit in the Struggles of People for Liberation and Fullness of Life," 275.

with how to go about presenting a feminist recasting of Trinitarian theology. She notes that the traditional process ordinarily begins with the Father, then the Son, and finally the Holy Spirit. While this approach is noted for its logic and organization, it renders a vision of God seemingly remote "from the historical experience of the Triune God in the economy of salvation and therefore from the actual life of believing persons."[39] Having in mind this traditional approach as she began her work, Johnson ultimately found that "feminist consciousness subverted it in an irresistible way."[40] This consciousness, rooted as it is in the centrality of women's experiences, moved Johnson to begin her exploration of the Trinity where Divine Livingness dwells, "where the dialectic of presence and absence shapes life in all its struggle"[41]—in the experience of the Holy Spirit in the world's history.

This point of departure, according to Johnson, commends itself in a variety of ways. By attending to the religious experiences of women unbounded by ecclesial strictures, Johnson can dwell in the prophetic and experiential climes in which the Spirit of God thrives, which has the potential to generate more creative encounters with the mystery of the Holy Spirit. Finally, this method roots theological reflection within the world's history, the very place wherein God first revealed Godself as Trinity and wherein God will continue to do so in experiential and comprehensible ways.

Johnson indicates that there are three specific categories within the world's history that mediate the Spirit's presence: the natural world, personal and interpersonal experience, and systemic structures. Despite these wide-ranging spheres of divine presence, the Spirit has frequently been narrowly institutionalized in ecclesial structures, privatized in personal piety, overlooked in favor of divine transcendence, and neglected through lack of personal imagery. Seeking to rectify these conditions, Johnson mines a variety of Biblical and rabbinical images that have an already established female resonance. From these, she retrieves the traditions of Spirit, *Shekinah*,[42]

---

39   Johnson, *She Who Is*, 121.

40   Johnson, *She Who Is*, 121.

41   Johnson, *She Who Is*, 121.

42   In the early rabbinic sources, the *Shekhinah* connoted the personification

and Wisdom/Sophia. The Biblical and rabbinical traditions have already been rendered with female personifications and have represented them with names that are grammatically female: *ruah* (Spirit), *Shekinah* (Divine Indwelling), and *hokmah/Sophia* (Wisdom). After assessing whether these symbols had robust enough potential to bear the image of God in terms of women's experiences, Johnson chose the figure of Sophia in the Wisdom tradition[43] and applied it to speak of Sophia-God in a Trinity of Persons as Mother-Sophia, Jesus-Sophia, and Spirit-Sophia.[44] The present purpose calls for a focus on Spirit-Sophia.

Supported by multiple citations from Scripture, Johnson characterizes the actions of Spirit-Sophia as those of vivifying, renewing, empowering, and gracing. Sophia introduces herself as *Creator Spiritus* in Proverbs 8:

> When [God] established the heavens, I was there,
> when he drew a circle on the face of the deep, when he made firm the skies above,
> when he established the fountains of the deep, when he assigned to the sea its limit,
> so that the waters might not transgress his command,
> when he marked out the foundations of the earth,
> then I was beside him, like an artisan; and I was daily his delight,
> rejoicing before him always, rejoicing in his inhabited world
> and delighting in the children of earth.
> Proverbs 8:26–31

---

and hypostatization of God's presence in the world, of God's immanence and immediacy in a specific place on earth. The Talmud referred to the *Shekhinah* as the visible and audible manifestation of God's presence on earth as well as the omnipresence and activity of God in the world. For a more expansive treatment, see Gloria L. Schaab, "The Power of Divine Presence: Toward a *Shekhinah* Christology," in *Christology: Memory, Inquiry, Practice: Proceedings of the College Theology Society 2002*, ed. Anne Clifford and Anthony Godzieba, 92–115. Maryknoll, NY: Orbis, 2003.

43 References can be found in the Books of Wisdom, of Proverbs, and of Sirach.

44 Johnson, *She Who Is*, 124–33.

Through the Spirit's *vivifying* energy, "The world comes into being and remains in being through divine creative power."[45] As *renewing* and *empowering*, Spirit-Sophia "renews the face of the earth" (Psalm 104:3) and transforms political structures. Those who rule are counseled to seek her, and she promises to be readily found.

> Wisdom is radiant and unfading,
> and she is easily discerned by those who love her, and is found by those who seek her.
> She hastens to make herself known to those who desire her.
> He who rises early to seek her will have no difficulty, for he will find her sitting at
> his gates.
> To fix one's thought on her is perfect understanding,
> and he who is vigilant on her account will soon be free from care,
> because she goes about seeking those worthy of her,
> and she graciously appears to them in their paths and meets them in every thought.
> (Wisdom 6:12–16)

To those who are unjust, however, Spirit-Sophia speaks a critical word of prophecy and empowers human liberation from injustice.

> Spirit-Sophia inspires human creativity and joy in the struggle. Wherever the gift of healing and liberation in however partial a manner reaches the winterized or damaged earth, or peoples crushed by war and injustice, or individual persons weary, harmed, sick, or lost on life's journey, there the new creation in the Spirit is happening.[46]

Even as the world groans, waiting for redemption (Romans 8:22), Spirit-Sophia galvanizes the human community to act with justice and hope in the face of suffering—from sexism, racism, poverty, and violence. Like a midwife, she brings forth new life, "shaping the world toward its ultimate end: the liberation of the world in God."[47] Through divine grace, Spirit-Sophia draws human beings toward Holy Mystery, shapes the life of the community, and empowers mission.

---

45   Johnson, *She Who Is*, 133.

46   Johnson, *She Who Is*, 135.

47   Johnson, *She Who Is*, 138.

Johnson's creative appropriation of the image of the Spirit-Sophia leads to "three key insights important for feminist theology of God: the transcendent God's immanence, the divine passion for liberation, and the constitutive nature of relation."[48] In contrast to notions found in classical theism, Spirit-Sophia is not simply remote and beyond the world, but indwelling and pervasive, a participant in the world's "fragility, chaos, tragedy, fertility, and beauty."[49]

> Though she is but one, she can do all things,
> and while remaining in herself, she renews all things;
> in every generation she passes into holy souls
> and makes them friends of God, and prophets;
> for God loves nothing so much as the one who lives with wisdom.
>
> (Wisdom 7:27–28)

Rather than impassable and neutral in response to the world's conflicts, Spirit-Sophia is "biased in favor of life's flourishing...and bound to compassion for the world."[50] Thus, Spirit-Sophia is at once intrinsically related, yet essentially free.

> Relationality is intrinsic to her very being as love, gift, and friend both to the world and within the holy mystery of God.... In fact, her ways of operating signal that far from being contradictory these two elements, freedom and relation, are essential to one another and enhance one another in a correlative way: "While remaining in herself, she renews all things" (Wisdom 7:27).[51]

Through the symbol of Spirit-Sophia, women's reality is demonstrated to be *capax Dei*, capable of bearing and symbolizing the Divine Mystery. Furthermore, the Sophia paradigm has the capacity for expansion beyond the activities of the vivifying and gracing Spirit of God to the full participation and presence of God in human history, incarnate in a

---

48   Johnson, *She Who Is*, 147.

49   Johnson, *She Who Is*, 147.

50   Johnson, She Who Is, 147.

51   Johnson, *She Who Is*, 148.

particular way in Jesus of Nazareth. For this reason, the divine image of Spirit-Sophia is not liberative and redemptive solely for women, but rather for the human community as a whole. By her being and actions, Spirit-Sophia refutes an image of God as distant and unrelated, as well as the narrow image of women as partially human and less than divine. As Johnson stresses, in the end,

> [These] theological motifs about the Spirit play off one another to hint at the reality of the mystery of God to whom the universe owes its very breath but whom we never comprehend. What is intellectual darkness, however, emits existential light, once it is understood that the world is held in existence by her compassionate power while human beings are challenged to be allies of her liberating grace.[52]

A LOOK AHEAD

The insights raised by the feminist, womanist, and mujerista theologians in this chapter are seldom reflected in the writings of their male counterparts within contemporary contextual pneumatologies. Nonetheless, Black and Latinx theologians have made their own critical contributions to the expansion of thought on the Holy Spirit from their respective cultural and social experiences. The next chapter examines pneumatologies arising from the African-American experience in the United States through the writings of James Cone, J. Deotis Roberts, and David Emmanuel Goatley.

FOR REFLECTION

- Reflect on your experience of the Holy Spirit as compassionate presence and liberating grace. What was their impact on you? To what did they motivate you?
- How does Spirit-Wisdom—as giver of life, as maternal face of God, and as proclaimer of justice—resonate in your life? Name experiences associated with each.

---

52   Johnson, *She Who Is*, 149.

- In what ways might the creative power of the Spirit be making you aware of your own dignity or of the contradiction between what is and what should or could be in your life? Name them for further reflection.

FOR FURTHER READING

Barbosa, Patricia Urueña. "The Holy Spirit and Gender Equality: A Latin American Perspective." *Vision* 13:1 (Spring 2012): 40–47.

Bergin, Helen. "Feminist Pneumatology." *Colloquium* 42:2 (2010): 188–207.

Brown, John P. "The Holy Spirit in the Struggles of People for Liberation and Fullness of Life." *International Review of Mission* 79:315 (1990): 273–81.

Johnson, Elizabeth A. "Spirit-Sophia," 121–49. In *She Who Is: The Mystery of God in Feminist Theological Discourse*. New York: Crossroad, 1992.

Thomas, Linda. "The Holy Spirit and Black Women." In *Christian Doctrines for Global Gender Justice*, ed. Jenny Daggers and Grace Ji-Sun Kim, 73–78. New York: Palgrave Macmillan, 2015.

The Power of God

The Holy Spirit in Black Theology

INTRODUCTION

IN HIS BOOK *BLACK Theology and Black Power*, James Cone wrote that "God's manifestation as Spirit is indispensable for a total picture of the Christian God.... The Holy Spirit is the power of God at work in the world effecting in the life of his people his intended purposes."[1] Nonetheless, Danté Quick, in his essay "Toward a Black Pneumatology," asserts that "Black Theology lacks a holistic pneumatology adept at offering insight into the Spirit's capacity to offer the internal structure of strength capable of engaging in external liberative activity."[2] A review of the literature, moreover, seems to bear out Quick's contention. While there is a significant amount of writing on the Holy Spirit from the perspective of the Black church, Black spirituality, and eschatological liberation, there is far less systematic writing on the liberative activity of the Holy Spirit in the Black community.

This chapter focuses on the writings of three Black theologians and their insights into the work of the Spirit in Black communities. It is important to note that Black liberation theologies and pneumatologies

---

1   James Cone, *Black Theology and Black Power* (Maryknoll, NY: Orbis, 2018), 64.

2   Danté Ronald Quick, "Toward a Black Pneumatology: An Exploration of the Holy Spirit via the Theologies of Howard Washington Thurman, Martin Luther King, Jr., and Kelly Brown Douglas," unpublished dissertation, Graduate Theological Union, Berkeley, CA, September 2017, 4.

arise from within the United States in response to racism and oppression of the Black community. These have deep and tangled roots in the United States dating back to the forcible importation of slaves more than four hundred years ago. The theologies and pneumatologies written from this hermeneutical context identify themselves with the concerns of Black men and women in America and seek to empower the Black community to recognize and break the chains of oppression that bind it. It is firmly grounded in the belief "that the liberation of the black community *is* God's liberation."[3] While pneumatological writings are not extensive, stemming from a predominant focus on Christology within the Black context, that makes it all the more necessary to mine those writings on the Holy Spirit and liberation that do exist from Black theologians.

Noteworthy among these and presented first in this chapter is the work of James Cone on the Holy Spirit from his classic text *Black Theology and Black Power.* Cone quite clearly situates the Spirit's liberative activities in the crux of the Black community's existential struggle and suffering. This is followed by an explicitly liberative treatment of the Holy Spirit from a Black perspective by theologian J. Deotis Roberts. In his work, Roberts focuses on social conscience and social justice "in the power of the Spirit."[4] Finally, this chapter engages the insights of David Emmanuel Goatley in his article "The Improvisation of God: Toward an African American Pneumatology." After exploring understandings of the Holy Spirit as community with God and as the power of God, Goatley offers the creative proposal of the Holy Spirit as the improvisation of God in dialogue with the music of jazz.[5]

---

3   James Cone, *A Black Theology of Liberation* (Maryknoll, NY: Orbis, 2010), 5, emphasis in original.

4   J. Deotis Roberts, "The Holy Spirit and Liberation: A Black Perspective," *Mid-Stream* 24:4 (October 1985): 398–410.

5   David Emmanuel Goatley, "The Improvisation of God: Toward an African American Pneumatology," *Memphis Theological Seminary Journal* 33:1 (Spring 1995): 3–13.

THE POWER OF THE SPIRIT

James Cone: The Holy Spirit and Black Power

In his text *Black Theology and Black Power*, James Cone, often considered the father of the Black liberation theology movement, quotes from Eduard Schweizer concerning the power of the Spirit: "The spirit of God is power, power with a moral emphasis."[6] Rather than individual piety or prompting, Schweizer continues, the Spirit is "active power, that is to say, it is the personal activity of God's will, achieving a moral and religious object."[7] This, from Cone's perspective, highlights a mistake in the Church. Rather than "private moments of ecstasy or...individual purification from sin," Cone asserts that "the working of God's Spirit in the life of the believer means an involvement in the world where men are suffering."[8] When the Spirit takes hold of an individual, that one becomes "repelled by suffering and death caused by the bigotry of others...[that says] we need more time before black men can have human dignity."[9]

> The man possessed by God's Spirit has no time to ask abstract questions about how the poor got to be poor or why blacks are hated by whites.... Like John Brown who "lived and breathed justice," the man of the Spirit can only say, "Racism is evil, kill it!"[10]

Cone insists that for those of the Spirit, racism is not simply a word, but rather "a ghetto, poverty" that stimulates those impelled by the Spirit to "take sides with the sufferer" to become "the vehicle of the activity of God himself."[11]

---

6   Eduard Schweizer, "Spirit of God," *Bible Key Words: Faith and Spirit of God*, Vol. III (New York: Harper and Row, 1960), 2.

7   Schweizer, "Spirit of God," 2.

8   Cone, *Black Theology*, 65.

9   Cone, *Black Theology*, 65.

10   Cone, *Black Theology*, 65.

11   Cone, *Black Theology*, 66.

Citing Matthew 25, Cone asserts that the work of the Spirit in an individual is not always a conscious event. Like those in the parable who were taken aback when identified by God with those who had ministered to the neighbor, actions for justice may be motivated by the suffering of the poor and afflicted with little consciousness of the action of the Spirit. Regardless of whether one is conscious of God or not, "Authentic living according to the Spirit means that one's will becomes God's will, one's actions become God's action.... And to the extent that it is genuinely concerned and seeks to meet the needs of the oppressed, it is the work of God's Spirit."[12]

This raises the question for Cone of how a believer can be certain that he or she is possessed by the Spirit, or that he or she is doing the work of God. While there is no objective scale upon which this can be measured, Cone assures the believer that one knows when one is "in touch with the Real."[13] Rather, "It is an existential certainty that grips the whole of one's being in such a way that now all actions are done in the light of the Ultimate Reality."[14] Citing the work of William Hordern, Cone states:

> There are no rational tests to measure this quality of being grasped in the depths of one's being. The experience is its own evidence, the ultimate datum. To seek for a higher evidence, a more objective proof—such as the Bible, the Fathers, or the Church—implies that such evidence is more real than the encounter itself.... [There] is nothing the Christian can point to that is more convincing than the relationship itself. The relationship itself carries with it its own power to convince.[15]

Because of his existential commitment to the Black community, Cone identifies the power of the Spirit with Black Power, "God's new

---

12 Cone, *Black Theology*, 67.

13 Cone, *Black Theology*, 67.

14 Cone, *Black Theology*, 68.

15 Cone, *Black Theology*, 68; cf. William Hordern, *Speaking of God* (New York: Macmillan, 1964), 176.

way of acting in America."[16] He admits that the encounter with Black power, especially as God's power, may be a "terrible experience" for whites and even some blacks. "Like the people of Jesus's day, they will find it hard to believe that God would stoop so low as to reveal himself in and through Black people and especially the 'undesirable elements.'"[17] According to Cone, however, that is the point. God as Spirit encounters persons "at that level of experience which challenges their being."[18] As a result, Cone insists, there is no spirit in American life that challenges individuals as the spirit of Black power. This is a spirit that has educational implications, political consequences, and economic ramifications. Because of this, Cone claims, "Such a spirit is not merely compatible with Christianity; in America in the latter twentieth century it is Christianity."[19]

As a result, Cone understands the Church as "that people called into being by the power and love of God to share in his revolutionary activity for the liberation of man."[20] It consists of a people seized by the Holy Spirit, constituted by that Spirit, and living according to that Spirit in Christ. From the call of Abraham, to the election of Israel, to the coming of Christ, Christianity in its religious history not only preaches a word of liberation but joins Christ in the work of liberation. For the Church to be relevant, Cone declares, it must join Christ in the Black revolution and catch the spirit of Black power.[21] Because of its "heritage of radical involvement with the world,"[22] the Black church must "accept its role as the sufferer."[23] As a result, Cone declares, "It may not only redeem itself through God's Spirit, but the white church as well."[24]

---

16   Cone, *Black Theology*, 69.

17   Cone, *Black Theology*, 69.

18   Cone, *Black Theology*, 69.

19   Cone, *Black Theology*, 71.

20   Cone, *Black Theology*, 71.

21   Cone, *Black Theology*, 126.

22   Cone, *Black Theology*, 127.

23   Cone, *Black Theology*, 128.

24   Cone, *Black Theology*, 128.

J. Deotis Roberts: The Holy Spirit and Human Liberation

J. Deotis Roberts, professor of philosophical theology, began his reflection on the Holy Spirit in a 1985 article by recounting a letter he had received, asking the following challenging questions: "Why are not liberation theologians writing about the Holy Spirit? Is there no spirit talk among the liberation theologians, Black feminists or Latin Americans?"[25] The author of that letter would certainly have been pleased with the resurgence in interest in the Holy Spirit in the years since then. Nonetheless, at that time, Roberts took up the challenge to focus his thought concerning human liberation in the context of its relationship with the Holy Spirit. Like many theologians in different contexts, Roberts was candid about the fact that little systematic attention had been directed toward the question of the Holy Spirit and liberation. Nonetheless, as this book demonstrates, liberation has become a predominant hermeneutic for the dynamic of liberation that yearns for a more extensive and systematic approach.

Roberts frames his pneumatological exploration around the question, "What is the connection between *charismata* and personal and social transformation?"[26] He points out that African-Afro-American religious understanding is holistic and thus does not entertain the personal-social, physical-spiritual dichotomies, noting instead "an assumed interpenetration in both instances."[27] Therefore, any discussion of the Holy Spirit in terms of presence or power in the Black church tradition must be cognizant of this perspective. Nonetheless, Roberts calls for a focused discussion of the presence and power of the Spirit specifically from a concern for the "socio-eco-politico aspects of liberation," emphasizing that "the true spirit of God bears clearly discernable 'fruits' in the life of the believer."[28]

According to Roberts, any discussion of pneumatology must include Christology and cites a "double relation" between the Spirit and Christ

---

25 Roberts, "The Holy Spirit and Liberation: A Black Perspective," 398.

26 Roberts, "The Holy Spirit and Liberation: A Black Perspective," 398.

27 Roberts, "The Holy Spirit and Liberation: A Black Perspective," 398.

28 Roberts, "The Holy Spirit and Liberation: A Black Perspective," 399.

elucidated by Hendrikus Berkhof in his book, *The Doctrine of the Holy Spirit.*[29]

> In the first instance the Spirit is said to have a priority over against Jesus.
> Jesus is described as the bearer of the Spirit. The Synoptic Gospels point up
> this relation between Jesus and the Spirit. In accordance with the proph-
> ecies it was expected that the Spirit would rest upon the Messiah. The
> Messiah was referred to as the Anointed One because God had anointed
> him with his Spirit. This association of the presence and power of the Spirit
> with Jesus is illustrated by passages in Matthew, Luke and Acts.[30]

However, Berkhof indicates that this priority is somewhat reversed
in the writings of Paul and John. In these, the Spirit is discussed as
the Spirit of Christ, who in turn sends the Spirit, breathes out the
Spirit, and transmits the Spirit as the Risen Christ. Following Berkhof,
Roberts sees these two relations as complementary:

> Jesus is the sender of the Spirit because he has first been the receiver and
> bearer of the Spirit.... Jesus is conceived by the Spirit, guided by the spirit,
> filled with the Spirit. The Spirit rests on Jesus and goes out from Jesus. The
> one on whom the Spirit remains, baptizes with the holy spirit.[31]

As a result, Roberts insists that Christology must be viewed pneumatologically and, conversely, that pneumatology must always be regarded
in relation to Christology. "The Spirit descends like a Dove, but He
also comes as Wind and Fire," Roberts writes. But like the anointed
one, Jesus of Nazareth, those possessed of and by the Spirit are called
"to liberate from oppressed conditions like racism and poverty."[32]

As indicated at the outset of this chapter, and in the work of Cone
above, pneumatology from the Black theological perspective tends to
focus on the power of the Spirit acting in the Black church. Roberts
emphatically points out the centrality of the Spirit in the Black church

---

29   Hendrikus Berkhof, *The Doctrine of the Holy Spirit* (Atlanta, GA: John Knox Press,
     1976), 13–14.

30   Roberts, "The Holy Spirit and Liberation: A Black Perspective," 400.

31   Roberts, "The Holy Spirit and Liberation: A Black Perspective," 401.

32   Roberts, "The Holy Spirit and Liberation: A Black Perspective," 407.

tradition, while bemoaning the dearth of systematic theological focus on the doctrine of the Spirit by Black theologians. He urges a deep consideration and development of not only the current scholarship of Pentecostal theologians in this regard, but also of the African roots of Pentecostalism, with its impact on Black Pentecostal expression. Nevertheless, Roberts contends that the starting point for reflection on the relation between the Spirit and the Church must always be "the primitive Christian Church and the witness of the Spirit in the whole Church of Christ."[33]

From Roberts's perspective, the church is a "creation of the Spirit" and, as such, is both institution and community. However, while related, there is a distinction between the two. "Institutions belong to the world of structures. Communities belong to the world of persons."[34] Furthermore, the community of persons expresses itself as an *Event*, energized by the Spirit.

> *Institute* refers to established relationships and patterns of historical and social order—stable forms and definite structures. *Event* points to the energizing of the church by the Spirit, the spontaneous quality of the human response and the character of the community's life of grace. The *Event* is foundational. The institutional elements are the result and the vessel for the event.[35]

Within the church, moreover, the interrelationship between the Spirit and Christ accented by Roberts becomes tangible and is extended beyond the church to the world. "In Word, sacraments and ministry, Christ is made present to the community of his church. This community in its turn is called to be the means by which Christ is made present to the world."[36] Thus, while integral to the Black church, the church community itself is not the last aim of the Holy Spirit's influence; that aim is "humankind as a whole." To achieve this aim, "the Spirit draws

---

33   Roberts, "The Holy Spirit and Liberation: A Black Perspective," 407.

34   Roberts, "The Holy Spirit and Liberation: A Black Perspective," 408.

35   Roberts, "The Holy Spirit and Liberation: A Black Perspective," 408, italics in original.

36   Roberts, "The Holy Spirit and Liberation: A Black Perspective," 408.

wider and wider circles around Christ," accomplishing through the church God's desires and purposes for the world. This outreach, this extension, this ever-widening circle of the Spirit's activity enables the Black church to connect and integrate church as *event* with church as *institute*. "The Black church...operating in the power of the Spirit... moves from worship to social involvement,"[37] as demonstrated through the life and work of the Rev. Martin Luther King, Jr. Reminiscent of the perspective of James Cone's Spirit as Black power, Roberts states:

> It is consistent with the Black church tradition to assert that the same Spirit which is present when the community is "gathered" also sends Black Christians forth to claim their humanity. The spirit that comforts and heals in Black worship, renews and empowers us as we oppose the evils in the society which would humiliate and destroy us.[38]

Thus, once again, pneumatology is about liberation in *history*, in the *real lives of human beings*. Roberts affirms that Black Christians are not simply concerned about what happens *within* each person; Black Christians are concerned about what the presence and power of the Holy Spirit does *between* persons. Citing the Beatitudes and the fruits of the Spirit in the letter to the Galatians 5, Roberts proposes that Black Christians have "perceived that the Holy Spirit of God seems to have the greatest interest in relationships between human beings."[39] As a result, in the words of Samuel Rayan, "The Holy Spirit is in truth the Father of the poor, the one who is really concerned with the less fortunate and the marginated."[40] In the tradition of the Black church, the Holy Spirit not only heals, but also empowers persons to strive for liberation from oppression and to hasten the coming of God's reign.

> In sum, in the Black church tradition, the Spirit is not merely a Dove, but Wind and Fire also. The Comforter is also the Strengthener. Justice in the social order, no less than joy and peace in the hearts of believers, is for the

---

37   Roberts, "The Holy Spirit and Liberation: A Black Perspective," 408.

38   Roberts, "The Holy Spirit and Liberation: A Black Perspective," 409.

39   Roberts, "The Holy Spirit and Liberation: A Black Perspective," 409.

40   Samuel Rayan, *The Holy Spirit* (Maryknoll, NY: Orbis, 1978), 137.

Black church evidence of the Spirit's presence and power.[41]

David Emmanuel Goatley: "The Improvisation of God"

"African-American Christians are thoroughly trinitarian," asserts David Emmanuel Goatley. "The theological language of black Christians reveals a trinitarian conceptualization of God in which God is referred to as Father, Son, and Spirit interchangeably in prayers, songs, and sermons." At the same time, however, Goatley insists on the "crucial role" of the Holy Spirit in the lives of African-American Christians. Hence, the conflation of trinitarian persons in the African-American spiritual and liturgical tradition requires "more substantive reflection" concerning African-American pneumatology.[42]

In his essay "The Improvisation of God: Toward an African-American Pneumatology," Goatley explores three hermeneutical approaches to understanding the Holy Spirit. Two of these approaches—The Holy Spirit as Community with God and The Holy Spirit as the Power of God—are well grounded in the African-American Christian consciousness and experience. The third approach that Goatley considers is a novel interpretation of the Holy Spirit as the Improvisation of God, which he contends is "authentic to the African-American culture and consistent with the biblical tradition."[43]

THE HOLY SPIRIT AS COMMUNITY WITH GOD

In African-American Christianity, the Holy Spirit has a dual communal function: the Spirit enables people to experience community with God as well as with others who belong to God. Goatley suggests that this experience reflects the resistance of African and African diaspora persons to dichotomize "concept and experience, thought and life."[44] According to Goatley, this intersection between the human and the spirit world demonstrated the influence of the traditional religion of

---

41   Roberts, "The Holy Spirit and Liberation: A Black Perspective," 410.

42   Goatley, "The Improvisation of God," 3.

43   Goatley, "The Improvisation of God," 4.

44   Goatley, "The Improvisation of God," 4.

Africa, which held a deep belief that "the individual and the community were continuously involved with the spirit world in the practical affairs of daily life."[45] From the West African perspective, God as Spirit was envisioned as both transcendent power and immanent presence, "constant among humanity and...involved with the affairs of God's creation."[46] This is symbolized in West African theology through a god known as *Elegba*, or *Legba*, "who brought divinity to earth, intervening in people's lives and serving as a messenger of the gods."[47]

According to Goatley, the conceptual link between Legba and the Holy Spirit helped to forge a link between the natural and the supernatural in the African-American religious awareness, "a logical conceptualization of the simultaneity [between] the other world and this world."[48] As a result, states theologian Diana Hayes, African-American Christians are "returning to their roots in the African American community—a community brought into existence by the action of the Spirit, shaping, forming, nurturing, and sustaining an oppressed and beleaguered people."[49] Hayes's conjunction between the work of the Spirit and the oppressed African-American community highlights for Goatley the reality that "community without commitment to social justice is a theological oxymoron."[50] He draws on the work of J. Deotis Roberts, quoted above, to assert that "the spirit that comforts and heals in Black worship, renews and empowers us as we oppose the evils in the society which would humiliate and destroy us."[51] In Goatley's estimation, this understanding becomes a bridge between the pneumatological concepts of community and power.

---

45   Gayraud S. Wilmore, *Black Religion and Radicalism: An Interpretation of the Religious History of Afro-American Peoples*, 2nd ed. (Maryknoll, NY: Orbis, 1983), 15.

46   Goatley, "The Improvisation of God," 5.

47   Goatley, "The Improvisation of God," 5.

48   Goatley, "The Improvisation of God," 6.

49   Diana Hayes, "Slain in the Spirit: Black American and the Holy Spirit," *Journal of the Interdenominational Theological Center* 20:1–2 (1992–93): 108.

50   Goatley, "The Improvisation of God," 7.

51   Roberts, "The Holy Spirit and Liberation," 409.

THE HOLY SPIRIT AS THE POWER OF GOD

In the African consciousness, Goatley contends, power is not conceived as "some metaphysical impersonal force," but rather as "a personal imperative element in human existence."[52] In the words of Allan Anderson,

> In the holistic African worldview we may not adopt a Western dualistic idea that the power of the Spirit only has to do with some sort of mystical inner power and nothing with our concrete physical, social, political and economic needs. God loves and desires the welfare of the whole person; and so he sends his Spirit to bestow a divine, liberating ability and strength which enables a person to continue.[53]

Goatley perceives this interpretation of the Spirit as power as "energizing," as opposed to those pneumatologies that fail to address the suffering and oppression of people. "There is the need for power which addresses the essential needs of life as well as offers shelter from life's dangers and disappointment."[54]

To emphasize the nature of Spirit as power, Goatley once again engages the thought of J. Deotis Roberts, as well as that of James Cone and Robert Hood. Goatley accents Roberts's points that the Holy Spirit imparts spiritual life, supplies comfort, provides guidance, and imbues with strength those who are suffering.[55] In addition, he highlights the insights of James Cone from *Black Theology and Black Power*, in which Cone maintains that the Spirit is imparted to people to transform their lives and actions toward involvement with the suffering in ways that continue the work of God in Jesus Christ.[56] Finally, Goatley appropriates

---

52 Goatley, "The Improvisation of God," 8.

53 Allan Anderson, "Pentecostal Pneumatology and African Power Concepts: Continuity or Change," *Missionalia* 19:1 (1990): 68.

54 Goatley, "The Improvisation of God," 8.

55 J. Deotis Roberts, *Liberation and Reconciliation: A Black Theology*, rev. ed. (Maryknoll, NY: Orbis, 1994), 64.

56 Cone, *Black Theology and Black Power*, 57.

the insights of Robert E. Hood in his discussion of the Holy Spirit as power. According to Hood, the Spirit is "active and acting, engaged and engaging, an act and an event," empowering the struggle for liberation, facilitating solidarity, and relating religion to culture.[57] In so doing, it becomes clear that the spirituality permeating the Christian is not *imitati Christi* but *participati Christi*, through social action toward liberation, as well as in "performance, drama, emotion, and ritual."[58]

THE HOLY SPIRIT AS THE IMPROVISATION OF GOD

Hood's emphasis on performance becomes the impetus for Goatley's creative interpretation of the Holy Spirit as the improvisation of God. He points out that, in addition to melody, harmony, and rhythm, jazz music also features syncopation, improvisation, and inspiration. From these elements, Goatley appropriates improvisation or spontaneity as characteristic of the Holy Spirit. He clarifies the fact that improvisation or spontaneity is not impromptu; rather, it is that which "rises from a particular occasion" and is "on the verge of being worked out."[59] In this description, he sees a correspondence among improvisation, realized and unrealized eschatology, and sanctification, all within the unfolding mystery of the Holy Spirit of God.

According to Goatley, a key characteristic of the Holy Spirit is an intimate presence and involvement with humanity, such that God may be affected by God's creation and creatures. As a result, God is thoroughly involved with and responsive to humanity. Such involvement with and responsiveness to the object of one's attention and activity is especially characteristic of improvisation within jazz music. As Goatley indicates, "In African-American music...the performance of a...song is never performed precisely the same way twice."[60] As the performer engages the score, the performer becomes immanently involved in its creation and recreation, working out the performance with various

---

57   Robert E. Hood, *Must God Remain Greek: Afro Cultures and God-Talk* (Minneapolis: Fortress Press, 1990), 209.

58   Hood, *Must God Remain Greek*, 205.

59   Goatley, "The Improvisation of God," 10.

60   Goatley, "The Improvisation of God," 11.

nuances in response to a particular moment. And thus it is with the
Spirit of God.

> While God is consistent in Godself, and while we can expect God to act in
> certain ways…, God is not obligated to act in ways predicted or prescribed
> by humanity…. God can and does exceedingly abundantly more than we
> can think or ask. God never ceases to amaze and to surprise…. This, at
> heart, can be understood in terms of the improvisation of God.[61]

Clearly, improvisation entails a degree of expectancy, unpredictability,
and surprise. Goatley admits that improvisation may be frightening to
those who insist on a kind of consistency in God. Nonetheless, one can
never truly predict God's activity, and to do so would be presumptuous.
Rather, improvisation acknowledges "the absolute holiness and freedom of God, who plays a score, but supplies appropriate variation and
syncopation during the experience of the song according to the inspiration within God's own being."[62] Goatley maintains that the notion of
divine improvisation entails a fundamental harmony in the nature of
God; God operates within a predictable order within the "score" that
is not haphazard or confused. That said, improvisation also implies
the freedom of the Spirit, like the wind to be as it will. As Goatley
concludes:

> Improvisation means that God is free…. Improvisation means that God is
> free to be as the wind—blowing in the direction in which God chooses. God
> is free to succor and surprise, to comfort and create. Improvisation means
> that God is God, and that God will always be God.[63]

A LOOK AHEAD

As indicated at the beginning of this chapter, Black pneumatology is
an area of theological writing that stems from the experience of racism

---

61   Goatley, "The Improvisation of God," 11.

62   Goatley, "The Improvisation of God," 12.

63   Goatley, "The Improvisation of God," 13.

and oppression of the Black community in the United States. In like manner, the pneumatologies presented in the next chapter are situated in the Latinx context and arise from the experience of xenophobia and discrimination suffered by Latinx persons in the United States. The Latinx theologians in the next chapter take up the challenge of finding the Holy Spirit in the midst of these experiences with pneumatologies that address the marginalization of Latinx persons in the United States.

FOR REFLECTION

- What is the Spirit improvising in your life? Is there expectancy, unpredictability, or surprise? Is there a fundamental harmony in the experience?
- Since the Spirit descends like a dove, but also comes as wind and fire, which do you find most prominent in your life? To what action does each prompt you?
- If the Spirit of God is power with a moral emphasis, how is the Spirit challenging you to take a stance, an involvement in the world where many are suffering?

FOR FURTHER READING

Goatley, David Emmanuel. "The Improvisation of God: Toward an African American Pneumatology." *Memphis Theological Seminary Journal* 33:1 (Spring 1995): 3–13.

Hayes, Diana. "Slain in the Spirit: Black Americans and the Holy Spirit." *The Journal of the Interdenominational Theological Center* 20:1–2 (1992–93): 97–115.

Roberts, J. Deotis. "The Holy Spirit and Liberation: A Black Perspective." *Mid-Stream* 24:4 (October 1985): 398–410.

CHAPTER NINE

El Espíritu Santo—Latinamente

INTRODUCTION

PNEUMATOLOGIES ENGAGED IN *LATINAMENTE* address the experiences that arise from the life and marginalization of Hispanic/Latino persons in the United States. As a demographic group, Hispanic/Latinos in the United States comprise the youngest and fastest-growing segment of the population. According to 2019 statistics from the U.S. Census Bureau, more 60 million Hispanics reside in the United States and represent more than 18% of the population. This makes the United States the second-largest "Hispanic country" in the world, with only Mexico having a larger Hispanic population. Projections indicate that the Hispanic/Latino population will reach 128.8 million by 2060, which will constitute 31% of the U.S. population. Yet despite this growing population, millions of Hispanics in the United States experience xenophobia, along with its social, political, and economic disenfranchisement, in all quarters and at all levels of American society. The Latinx theologians in this chapter take up the task of finding the Holy Spirit in the midst of the lives and challenges of U.S. persons of Latinx origin.

However, at the outset of his "Theological Musings toward a Latina/o Pneumatology," Néstor Medina admits that, while Latinx[1] theologians have reconfigured the theological task in creative and transformational

---

1   While I will opt for the current scholarly usage *Latinx* to apply to a person of Latin American origin or descent as a gender-neutral alternative to Latino or Latina, I will retain the particular terminology selected by each of the theologians in his writing.

ways, "one would be hard pressed to find any substantial work dealing explicitly with the work and nature of the Spirit in Latina/o theology."[2] This is not to say that the Spirit and the Spirit's activity are absent since the Spirit is often linked to Christology and even Mariology in Latinx theology. Moreover, Medina does a marvelous service to the discipline with his essay highlighting contributions from Eldín Villafañe, Samuel Solivan, and Oscar Garcia-Johnson. Nonetheless, although those authors discuss many aspects of Christian life, they "line up with traditional approaches to theology that articulate the activity of the Spirit as incomprehensible outside of the work of Christ."[3] This reality prompted Medina to "tease out" more unique examples of the Spirit's activity among Latinos and Latinas that inspired the choices in this chapter.

Encouraged by Medina, this chapter mined the literature to present three liberative perspectives on pneumatology from the Latinx theological landscape. The first perspective, the Spirit as *convivencia*, is from Medina himself, taken from his essay "Theological Musings toward a Latina/o Pneumatology." It implies "a relational ethos of *en conjunto*; it makes explicit the Latina/o human formation of living life in relationship with others in the context of *lo cotidiano*."[4] The second pneumatology this chapter engages is that of Samuel Solivan in his essay "The Holy Spirit: A Pentecostal Perspective,"[5] in which he calls for the personalization of the Holy Spirit as critical to the fullness of humanity for Latina/o Pentecostals. Finally, it explores the work of Orlando Espín, who introduces Our Lady of Guadalupe as a cultural expression of devotion to the Holy Spirit.[6]

---

2   Néstor Medina, "Theological Musings toward a Latina/o Pneumatology," in *The Wiley Blackwell Companion to Latino/a Theology*, ed. Orlando Espín (Malden, MA: John Wiley and Sons, 2015), 174–89.

3   Medina, "Latina/o Pneumatology," 177.

4   Medina, "Latina/o Pneumatology," 181.

5   Samuel Solivan, "The Holy Spirit: A Pentecostal Perspective," in *Teología en Conjunto: A Collaborative Hispanic Protestant Perspective*, ed. José David Rodríguez and Loida I. Martell-Otero (Louisville, KY: Westminster John Knox, 1997), 50–65.

6   Orlando O. Espín, "Mary in Latino/a Catholicism: Four Types of Devotion," *New Theological Review* 23:3 (2010): 16–25.

NEUMATOLOGÍA LATINAMENTE

Néstor Medina: "Convivencia"

As indicated in the introduction, Néstor Medina's work provided a vital pathway to discovering the more systematically developed pneumatologies from the Latinx context. Moreover, he added to these offerings a creative pneumatological musing of his own, that of "*convivencia* as a unique lens for understanding and speaking about the Spirit" for Latina/o persons.[7] According to Medina, *convivencia* concerns the relational manner of living and sharing life *en conjunto*, which is the basis of human formation in the Latina/o community. He states that any understanding of the Holy Spirit must be shaped by the essence of Latina/o relationality. Thus, for Medina, "the act of living with and sharing life—encompassed in *convivir*—is an appropriate way to frame the activity of the Spirit among Latinas/o" and is so for at least three reasons: the reality of *sobre-vivencia*, the activity of fiesta, and the notion of *acompañamiento*.[8]

Sobre-Vivencia

According to Medina, *convivencia* has historically been contextualized within *sobre-vivencia*.

> That is, the Latina/o capacity to coexist and live with comes with the background of overcoming incredible odds in the midst of violence, discrimination, lack of opportunities, systemic exclusion/marginalization, and so on. Generally, Latinas/os cannot speak of convivencia in naïve ahistorical terms, but always within the dynamics of struggle for life.[9]

This does not imply that Latina/os do not experience the Holy Spirit within moments of joy or happiness; however, the encounter with the Spirit is most frequently experienced during times of suffering, pain, and hopelessness.[10] With Latina/os,

---

7   Medina, "Latina/o Pneumatology," 181.

8   Medina, "Latina/o Pneumatology," 181.

9   Medina, "Latina/o Pneumatology," 182.

10   Medina, "Latina/o Pneumatology," 182.

> The Spirit groans, moans, cries, and feels the pain together with the victims of exclusion, violence, and injustice.... [The] Spirit is also injured by those actions which run counter to divine intentions for life, equality, and love, and works to rectify what has gone wrong."[11]

In such times, the experience of the Holy Spirit is an empowering and energizing force that enables Latina/os to continue the struggle *en la lucha*.

> As people are empowered to survive, we encounter the Spirit as one who struggles for life. Stated differently, the very struggle for life is itself a window into the divine Spirit's struggle for life in this world. As Latinas/os struggle for life, they align themselves with the work of the Spirit.[12]

Fiesta

In the midst of *sobre-vivencia*, nonetheless, Latina/os continue to engage in *fiesta*, "not as an idealized romantic motif but tempered with the sobering awareness that fiestas are touched by violence and exclusion."[13] Medina asserts that, within the very "messiness of life," Latina/os find the Spirit present and active.

> Even when many Latinas/os feel as though there are no reasons to celebrate or hope, they refuse to cancel celebrating life with family and friends, all the while praying to God and hoping that in the near future things will get better. We see this determination in the multiple religious-cultural celebrations of *quinceañera*, *posadas*, pilgrimages, birthdays, and so on, all of which make explicit the aspirations of the people and their obstinate refusal to give up.[14]

This determination is inspired by *el Espiritu santo*, who inspires Latina/os to celebrate and rejoice, even in the midst of hardship and sorrow. Moreover, because of their own spirit of "interconnectedness, a *nosotros*

---

11   Medina, "Latina/o Pneumatology," 182.

12   Medina, "Latina/o Pneumatology," 182.

13   Medina, "Latina/o Pneumatology," 182.

14   Medina, "Latina/o Pneumatology," 182.

shaped by 'familial' relations,"[15] Latina/os often experience through the Spirit the restoration of relationships, a healing of woundedness, and the capacity to imagine new possibilities. According to Medina, the "grammar of relational interconnectedness" that is expressed in Latina/os' spirit and spirituality extends beyond the human family "as *convivencia* illustrates the very nature of the divine Spirit's impetus to enter into relationship with the rest of creation."[16]

> It is this Spirit who invites us to celebrate life in *convivencia*; the call to *convivencia* is simultaneously a form of protest against social structures that focus on individualism at the expense of community, and an eschatological and prophetic reorientation of the world.[17]

Acompañamiento

Following from this interconnectedness, Medina proposes that *convivencia* entails the act of *acompañamiento*. While rooted in Roberto Goizueta's *Caminemos con Jesús: Toward a Hispanic/Latino Theology of Accompaniment*,[18] Medina argues that the notion of *acompañamiento* needs to be augmented pneumatologically in order to avoid subordination to the work of Jesus. This accompaniment involves the agency of both humanity and Spirit. However, from the human perspective, "accompaniment describes the act of walking with the poor and placing oneself where the poor are by assuming the ethico-political consequences of such a life and by accompanying each other in a mutual struggle for survival"[19]; thus, *convivencia* is clearly a prerequisite. Referencing the work of Oscar Garcia-Johnson,[20] Medina declares:

---

15 Medina, "Latina/o Pneumatology," 182.

16 Medina, "Latina/o Pneumatology," 182.

17 Medina, "Latina/o Pneumatology," 183.

18 Roberto S. Goizueta, *Caminemos con Jesús: Toward a Hispanic/Latino Theology of Accompaniment* (Maryknoll, NY: Orbis, 1999).

19 Medina, "Latina/o Pneumatology," 184.

20 Oscar Garcia-Johnson, *The Mestizo/a Community of the Spirit: A Postmodern Latino/a Ecclesiology* (Eugene, OR: Pickwick, 2009).

"To be a human being is to be in relationship with others, in *convivencia*, and to be in relationship with others means to walk with them; it is to be *acompañado* and it means to *acompañar* another."[21]

Nonetheless, the human capacity for *acompañamiento* is not possible without the agency of the Holy Spirit. Rather, it entails the "inspiring, energizing, and empowering activity of the Spirit" to strengthen Latina/os for the act of accompaniment in the midst of suffering and hardship. Moreover, "the economic activity of the Spirit [extends] from creation to resurrection, to the birth of the church and the sustaining of creation," which draws attention to three aspects of the Spirit's *acompañamiento*.[22] First, from the moment of creation, the Spirit's *acompañamiento* sustains all creation and creates the opportunity for the encounter between the human and the Divine. Furthermore, from this presence of the Spirit in creation arises the possibility of the historical person of Jesus of Nazareth, since the Spirit was clearly involved in Jesus' conception, growth, and anointing of Jesus for mission. In fact, Medina contends that "it was because of the Spirit that Jesus was able to carry out his ministry and perform miracles. And after Jesus was killed, it was the Spirit that raised him from the dead. We can safely affirm that the entire Jesus event was first and foremost a pneumatological event."[23] Finally, Medina affirms, the Spirit that accompanied and animated Jesus is the very Spirit that was given to humanity to complete the mission that Jesus had begun, a mission with the goal of *acompañamiento* as the Spirit accompanied Jesus.

> The actualization of such accompaniment by the Spirit is what makes it possible for humans to encounter the divine...[to] live our *imago Dei* to the fullest.... For those who, because of discrimination, abuse, exploitation, and marginalization, have lost their humanity, relationship with God implies being empowered by the Spirit to reclaim it.[24]

---

21   Medina, "Latina/o Pneumatology," 184.

22   Medina, "Latina/o Pneumatology," 184.

23   Medina, "Latina/o Pneumatology," 184.

24   Medina, "Latina/o Pneumatology," 185.

Samuel Soliván: The Personalization of the Spirit and Human Diversity

The concern about loss of humanity with which Medina concludes is precisely the concern that Samuel Soliván takes up in his essay "The Holy Spirit—Personalization and the Affirmation of Diversity: A Pentecostal Hispanic Perspective."[25] According to Soliván, "The Holy Spirit as a person relates to us as persons. As persons we relate to the Spirit from specific points of reference—gender, language, culture, and social class, to name a few of the aspects that inform our relation to the Spirit."[26] It is for this reason that Soliván argues for the *personalization* of the Holy Spirit. A depersonalized Spirit, Soliván contends, cannot contribute to the affirmation and empowerment of *persons* in their particularity and diversity. Prompted by philosophical idealism, this depersonalization is evident in seminaries, churches, and theological conferences despite fifteen hundred years of Christian tradition. Hence, Soliván urges his readers to "test all such spirits to see if they be from God."[27]

According to Soliván, the personalization of the Spirit is critical for Hispanic American pneumatology "because the relationship of the Spirit to persons, in this case Latinas and Latinos who daily experience treatment as non-persons, can provide a transformative model of personhood and self-esteem."[28] Hispanic persons are at the mercy of those who seek to dehumanize and objectify them, those "who employ a divine image to further their desire for control, who seek to domesticate the divine."[29] These dehumanizing powers and forces contradict the reality of the *imago Dei*, which is given through the agency of the Holy Spirit to all human persons. In this, the Holy Spirit is the image of

---

25 Samuel Soliván, "The Holy Spirit—Personalization and the Affirmation of Diversity: A Pentecostal Hispanic Perspective," in *Teología en Conjunto: A Collaborative Hispanic Protestant Theology*, ed. José David Rodríguez and Loida I. Martell-Otero (Louisville: Westminster John Knox Press, 1997), 50–65.

26 Soliván, "The Holy Spirit," 50.

27 Soliván, "The Holy Spirit," 51.

28 Soliván, "The Holy Spirit," 53.

29 Soliván, "The Holy Spirit," 53.

the personhood of the Trinity, "a communion of persons, not of influences or energies."[30] Jesus' own reference to the Holy Spirit as "another
advocate" reinforces the personhood of the Spirit, since it is clear that
Jesus is speaking of a personal presence. As a result, the relationship
between the Spirit and those who receive the Spirit is preserved as one
of person and subject, not subject and object.

As the personalized Spirit counteracts the non-personhood and
marginalization of Hispanic persons, so the Spirit heals the broken-
ness that results and enables both human and social transformation.[31]

> Nothing less than the full personhood of the Spirit is sufficient to reflect…
> the needs of the Hispanic community and the world. The Holy Spirit as gift
> of God and the bearer of gifts requires that we correct the present tendency
> toward pneumatological docetism. It is in both the personal and collective
> aspects of the Spirit that we come to know and experience the fullness of his
> person as gift, gift bearer, and rectifier.[32]

If the present tendency to depersonalize the Holy Spirit continues, it
will fail to counteract the dehumanization of the Hispanic community and to promote the restoration of its dignity as children of God.
Only the transforming power of the Holy Spirit, "bearer of the gifts of
wholeness, faith, hope, and love," can overcome oppression and usher
in a liberated future.[33]

From his primary focus on the Hispanic community, Soliván
expands his perspective from the Spirit's crucial role in the full
humanization of Hispanic persons. He further asserts that the personalized Spirit promotes and undergirds the cultural, ethnic, and lin-
guistic diversity of the Christian community. Through the Pentecost
event, Soliván states, the Spirit introduces "a counter paradigm to
those social constructions which functioned to separate diverse types
of people and communities from one another on the bases of race,

---

30   Soliván, "The Holy Spirit," 53.

31   Soliván, "The Holy Spirit," 54.

32   Soliván, "The Holy Spirit," 55.

33   Soliván, "The Holy Spirit," 55.

gender, language, and economic status."[34] He approaches this conclusion through a re-reading of Acts 2 to demonstrate its relevance
and affirmation of diversity within the contemporary Christian community. According to Solivàn, the inbreaking of the Holy Spirit on
Pentecost manifested that "in the order of creation and the order of
salvation," unity amid diversity was the divine intention in the sphere
of humanity and of creation.

The outpouring of the Spirit on the multitudes from many nations
and peoples at Pentecost demonstrated that the kingdom of God is
characterized by diversity, and so should the church today. Failure
to recognize this reality has led to oppression and prejudice of many
kinds—racism, sexism, and xenophobia—even among those who pur-
port to be Christian. "The fullness of the Spirit's presence and power
will be incomplete at best or absent," maintains Solivàn, "as long as we
continue to ignore or devalue the importance of the place of diversity
expressed through our culture, language, ethnicity, and gender."[35] The
tongues spoken on Pentecost were not those of angels but of a given
people; thus differences in culture or language must not serve as bar-
riers within communities of faith. Claims of superiority by any particular culture or race, therefore, are an affront to the Divine.

It is here that the two avenues of thought pursued by Solivàn converge. Personalization of the Holy Spirit is integral not only to the
flourishing humanity of the Hispanic community in particular, but also
to the community of faith comprised of persons of diverse languages,
cultures, ethnicities, and genders. Both are made possible by the power
of the Holy Spirit, who enables the Latina and Latino Americans and
all who are oppressed and dehumanized to liberate themselves as well
as their oppressors. Those who claim to be Spirit-filled, says Solivàn,
must also be Spirit-led and respond to the challenge "to incarnate...
collectively and individually, the ethic of love that directs us to love the
unlovely, to care for the stranger and the sojourner, and to extend hospitality to the foreigner and the sinner."[36]

---

34   Solivàn, "The Holy Spirit," 55.

35   Solivàn, "The Holy Spirit," 62.

36   Solivàn, "The Holy Spirit," 63.

Orlando Espín: La Virgen de Guadalupe and the Holy Spirit

In his chapter "An Exploration into the Theology of Grace and Sin" in
the book *From the Heart of Our People: Latino/a Explorations in Catholic
Systematic Theology*,[37] Orlando Espín explores a theme that has a
decided resonance with the thought of Leonardo Boff that was examined earlier in this text—namely, the association of the Holy Spirit with
the Virgin Mary. While each approaches his proposal differently and
thus comes to a different conclusion, the essence overlaps: Latino/a
popular religiosity toward *la Virgen* has less to do with Mary of Nazareth
than with the Holy Spirit. In fact, Sixto García suggests that Mary is
the "hermeneutical key" to the Trinitarian experience of the Holy
Spirit for Hispanic persons.[38] According to García, the "pneumatological symbol-reality of Mary" unveils the presence of the Holy Spirit in
Hispanic communities.[39] This insight of García's is profoundly echoed
by Virgilio Elizondo in his reflection on Our Lady of Guadalupe:

> The more I try to comprehend the intrinsic force and energy of the appari-
> tions of Our Lady of Guadalupe to Juan Diego in Tepeyac in 1531, at the very
> beginning of the Americas, the more I dare to say that I do not know of any
> other event since Pentecost that has had such a revolutionary, profound,
> lasting, far-reaching, healing, and liberating impact on Christianity.... I
> see her as the beginning of a new creation, the mother of a new humanity,
> and the manifestation of the femininity of God.... Our Lady of Guadalupe in
> not just another Marian apparition.[40]

It is on the basis of this remarkable apparition that Orlando Espín
constructs his pneumatology.

---

37 Orlando O. Espín and Miguel H. Diaz, eds., *From the Heart of Our People: Latino/a Explorations in Catholic Systematic Theology* (Maryknoll, NY: Orbis, 1999).

38 Sixto J. García, "A Hispanic Approach to Trinitarian Theology: The Dynamics of Celebration, Reflection, and Praxis," 107–32, in *We Are a People*, ed. Roberto Goizueta (Philadelphia: Fortress, 1992), 120.

39 García, "A Hispanic Approach," 124.

40 Virgilio Elizondo, *Guadalupe: Mother of the New Creation* (Maryknoll: Orbis, 1997), xi, 134.

Espín grounds his pneumatological insights in his understanding of the dialogical relationship between the Holy Spirit and culture. While the Holy Spirit is active within the encounter between the divine and human, all such mutual exchanges are culturally bound. For Latinos and Latinas in the United States, "the God and the grace experienced by Latinos/as are (necessarily!) culturally and socially contextualized...and expressive of the language, symbols, understandings, and images of the divine shaped by their culture, by their social place, and by the conflict underlying much of U.S. society."[41] For Espín, Latino/a devotion to Our Lady of Guadalupe is one such cultural expression of the experience of the Divine in their midst. This is the presupposition that focuses Espín's reflections on the apparition of Our Lady of Guadalupe.

In *From the Heart of Our People*, Espín begins his exposition with the clarification that he is not claiming that Mary is the Holy Spirit, a position that he considers "theologically impossible."[42] Moreover, he is not suggesting that Latino/a devotional expressions result from a lack of evangelization or a tendency toward syncretism.[43] What he is questioning is whether the apparition of Guadalupe is even representative of Mary of Nazareth at all. Instead, Espín reads the story of Guadalupe through the lens of pneumatology with the broader hope that it might open up "important new vistas in mainstream Christian theologies of the Holy Spirit."[44] Espín does so through a series of questions.

If the majority of Latinos/as (especially mature Latinas) relate to Guadalupe in ways that any mainstream Christian pneumatology would expect with respect to the Holy Spirit and if the people's expectations, "gifts" received, and explanations surrounding the Guadalupe devotion all seem to fit those that mainstream pneumatologies would associate with the Holy Spirit, is it unreasonable to question whether in fact we might not be dealing in the case of Guadalupe with the Holy Spirit?[45]

---

41 Espín, *From the Heart of Our People*, 134, emphasis in original.

42 Espín, *From the Heart of Our People*, 138.

43 Orlando O. Espín, "Mary in Latino/a Catholicism: Four Types of Devotion," *New Theological Review* 23:3 (2010): 24.

44 Espín, *From the Heart of Our People*, 138.

45 Espín, *From the Heart of Our People*, 138–39.

In a footnote to his work, Espín admits that, because of the
uniqueness of the Guadalupan apparition, such associations may be
a "historical fluke" that has no broader applicability to pneumatology.[46] Nonetheless, he continues to question why the symbols and language applied to the Holy Spirit must only be those of European origin.
Espín points out that the concept of the Holy Spirit was foreign to the
indigenous peoples despite the efforts of missionaries to the regions.
Catechetical materials such as the *Libro de Oraciones* depicted the Spirit
in typical European fashion as "a bird rising in flight, with a hat-like
halo on its head, and surrounded by lines that seem to communicate
radiant, glowing light."[47] According to Espín,

> Whatever their ultimate intention in this view [of Guadalupe as a Marian
> apparition], these colonial authors would have found it unacceptable
> to think of Guadalupe in other terms. They could have been accused of
> crypto-paganism, heresy or something to that effect, if they doubted that
> Guadalupe is just another way of referring to the mother of Jesus.[48]

This paucity of adequate symbolism or popular interpretation
prompts Espín to ask, "Couldn't the symbols and language associated
with Marian devotions, given the historical, cultural, and sociopolitical
events that profoundly rocked early colonial Mexico, have been 'trans-
ferred' by the recently conquered people to the still new (to them)
doctrine of the Holy Spirit?"[49] This is what happened, Espín points
out, with Wisdom and Logos with regard to Christology, so why is it not
possible that a similar "transfer" may have taken place to produce an
inculturated pneumatology in colonial Mexico? Furthermore, Espín
warns, if the insistence on Guadalupe as a Marian apparition remains,
"are we not granting 'normative' character to a dominant interpretation, that, in fact, is not the people's everyday own...[and] disre-
garding or dismissing the very 'popular' dimension in this important

---

46   Espín, *From the Heart of Our People*, 151.

47   Orlando O. Espín, *The Faith of the People* (Maryknoll, NY: Orbis, 1997), location
       (loc.) 1463.

48   Espín, *Faith of the People*, loc. 505.

49   Espín, *From the Heart of Our People*, 138.

component of popular Catholicism?"[50] Ultimately, Espín questions the core of the resistance to ascribing a pneumatological hermeneutic to Guadalupe when he asks whether there is something in the nature of the Divine that precludes its being imaged in feminine categories.[51]

The failure to entertain the possibility of a pneumatological interpretation of Guadalupe has significant pastoral and theological consequences. Focusing on the popular religiosity of Latinas, Espín asserts that "Mature Latinas would indeed claim that in and through Guadalupe they encounter and experience the God-who-is-for-us...as mother, as compassion, as power, as active and intimate presence, and as (re)creative/empowering energy,"[52] qualities traditionally applied to the Divine as Holy Spirit. Consistent with the pneumatologies of both Medina and Soliv1̇án, Espín concludes that, through the eyes of Latinas, Guadalupe is "the wise counselor, compassionate with all but especially with the weakest members of the community, empowering the people to continue fighting in the face of adversity, sharing their joys and sorrows, promoting solidarity, encouraging and supporting creative decisions, and making God's active presence and love felt and known within the lives of Latinos/as."[53] In all these ways, Espín contends, Latinas and Latinos *en lo cotidiano y en la lucha* encounter Our Lady of Guadalupe as an inculturated symbol of the Holy Spirit. Where such assertions will lead him, Espín is uncertain. "I can only guess," he admits, "and want to continue."[54]

A LOOK AHEAD

The final chapter of this book returns to that place where the Holy Spirit has been since the beginning: the cosmos as creation. The authors in

50   Espín, *Faith of the People*, loc. 522 and 531.

51   Note that feminist theologians would avoid the use of feminine, since it implies a cultural stereotype. The preferred usage is "female."

52   Espín, *From the Heart of Our People*, 139.

53   Espín, *From the Heart of Our People*, 139.

54   Espín, *Faith of the People*, loc. 548.

this text thus far have focused on the Spirit's presence and action in human life and experience—liberating, gracing, and transforming. How shall we recognize the Spirit's vivifying, renewing, creating action within the cosmos itself? The authors in this final chapter explore the variety of ways in which the Spirit, giver and sustainer of life, is continuously creative in, with, and under an evolving cosmos.

FOR REFLECTION

- Have you experienced the Spirit who "groans, moans, cries, and feels the pain" with you in your suffering? Reflect on the depth of that experience.
- How has the Holy Spirit dwelt with you in your particular gender, language, culture, or social class? How did you recognize this inculturated presence?
- When or where have you seen the "divine intention" of unity amid diversity lived out? In what way was the Spirit's presence palpable at that time?

FOR FURTHER READING

Elizondo, Virgilio. *Guadalupe: Mother of the New Creation*. Maryknoll, NY: Orbis, 1997.

Espín, Orlando O. "Mary in Latino/a Catholicism: Four Types of Devotion." *New Theological Review* 23:3 (2010): 16–25.

Medina, Néstor. "Theological Musings toward a Latina/o Pneumatology." In *The Wiley Blackwell Companion to Latino/a Theology*, ed. Orlando Espín, 174–89. Malden, MA: John Wiley and Sons, 2015.

Soliván, Samuel. "The Holy Spirit—Personalization and the Affirmation of Diversity: A Pentecostal Hispanic Perspective." In *Teología en Conjunto: A Collaborative Hispanic Protestant Theology*, ed. José David Rodríguez and Loida I. Martell-Otero, 50–65. Louisville: Westminster John Knox Press, 1997.

CHAPTER TEN

Spirit in the Cosmos

INTRODUCTION

IN THIS FINAL CHAPTER, the text shifts from its dedicated focus on the Personhood of the Holy Spirit in human experience to an exploration of the Spirit's manifestation in the broader cosmos. This movement away from Personhood does not imply that the Holy Spirit is less able to be experienced by human beings. It does, however, propose ways in which the Holy Spirit may be manifested through processes and structures that, while not necessarily personal, are nonetheless present, active, and liberative in the experience of individuals, societies, and the cosmos itself. Moreover, in his 1993 book *Toward a Theology of Nature*, theologian Wolfhart Pannenberg asserts, "If theologians want to conceive of God as creator of the real world, they cannot bypass the scientific description of that world."[1] In keeping with Pannenberg's claim, theologians in this chapter examine three manifestations of the Spirit in the cosmos, employing concepts drawn from ecological science and modern physics. The first is proposed by professor of environmental studies Mark I. Wallace in his examination of "The Green Face of God: Christianity in an Age of Ecocide," in which he considers "the Spirit enfleshed in creation" who "experiences the

---

1   Wolfhart Pannenberg, *Toward a Theology of Nature: Essays on Science and Faith* (Louisville, KY: Westminster John Knox, 1993), 33.

agony of an earth under siege."[2] The second contribution is that of theologian Wolfhart Pannenberg, who advances the image of the Holy Spirit as "field of force," drawn from modern physics, "as an analogy for the way ~~that~~ the Spirit works in the world and relates to all of nature."[3] Finally, I present my own proposal for considering the Holy Spirit as the Strange Attractor in an evolving cosmos who draws and integrates disparate aspects of cosmic and human life into greater unity, liberation, and love.[4] I have explored this concept through the notions of grace and of charism in a variety of my works until it finally dawned on me that both grace and charism are essentially manifestations of the Holy Spirit's very self.

COSMIC MANIFESTATIONS OF SPIRIT

Mark I. Wallace: "The Green Face of God"

Today, Mark Wallace begins, "We face an environmental crisis…of staggering proportions."[5] The issue for him is how to address this crisis in ways that will promote the sustenance and growth of human communities without impeding the survival and flourishing of non-human communities. Dismissing suggestions that this conundrum results from cognitive or technological failures, Wallace pinpoints the source as a spiritual one, "a failure to practice earth-healing [as] a matter of

---

2   Mark I. Wallace, "The Green Face of God: Christianity in an Age of Ecocide," *Cross Currents* 50:3 (Fall 2000): 310.

3   Theodore Whapham, "Spirit as Field of Force," *Scottish Journal of Theology* 67:1 (2014): 19.

4   See *Trinity in Relation: Creation, Incarnation, and Grace in an Evolving Cosmos* (Winona, MN: Anselm Academic Publishing, 2012); "Grace: The Strange Attractor in an Evolving Cosmos," *THEOFORUM* 43 (2012): 199–218; and "Charism: The 'Strange Attractor' in Religious Life," *The Occasional Papers* (A Publication of the Leadership Conference of Women Religious) 43:1 (2014): 6–8.

5   Wallace, "The Green Face of God," 311.

the heart."[6] It stems from humanity's inability to embrace our "co-belonging with nature.... That primordial sense of belonging to a whole web of life that our kind and otherkind need for daily sustenance."[7]

As a spiritual problem, moreover, Wallace points out the deleterious effects of many religious teachings that have led to the devastation of the Earth community. These include Christianity's dismissal of animistic traditions, stripping nature of its spiritual meaning, and the teaching that humans must exercise "dominion over the earth," too often distorted by human beings into a domination that views Earth as "our private possession."[8] Nonetheless, if Christianity is the impetus for ecological crisis, could it offer any possibilities for ecological healing? In answer to this question, Wallace retrieves the credal understanding of the Holy Spirit as Giver of Life, "the divine force within the cosmos who continually indwells and works to sustain all forms of life.... God's invigorating presence within the society of all living things."[9] The name that Wallace gives the Spirit as this divine presence is the "Green Face of God."

Regrettably, Wallace notes, the Holy Spirit is most often thought of as a "bodiless, immaterial reality, over and against the physical world, which is not the same nature as Spirit."[10] This often derives from the Western tendency not only to separate entities into binary oppositions—body/mind, matter/spirit, physical/spiritual—but also to rank the latter of the two hierarchically over the first. As a result, "Spirit is regarded as an eternally invisible and incorporeal force superior to the earthly realm which is mired in contingency and change."[11] Nonetheless, Wallace points out that much of Scripture does not support this dichotomous hierarchy and, in fact, envisions the Spirit as "creaturely life-form always already interpenetrated by the material world."[12]

---

6   Wallace, "The Green Face of God," 312.

7   Wallace, "The Green Face of God," 312.

8   Wallace, "The Green Face of God," 313.

9   Wallace, "The Green Face of God," 314.

10 Wallace, "The Green Face of God," 315.

11 Wallace, "The Green Face of God," 315.

12 Wallace, "The Green Face of God," 316.

Wallace demonstrates that the Scriptures "suffuse" the Spirit with imagery from nature: as vivifying breath, healing wind, living water, purgative fire, and divine dove.[13] Many of these, particularly the divine dove, have militated against the recognition of the Personhood of the Holy Spirit throughout the tradition. However, Wallace is attempting to put forth a complementary—rather than conflicting—notion of the *embodiment* of the Spirit within the created realm to emphasize the Spirit as "an earthly *lifeform* who labors to create, sustain, and renew humankind and otherkind in solidarity with one another."[14] In so doing, nature becomes the principal modality of the Spirit's presence and action in the world. "Now the earth's waters and winds and birds and fires will not be regarded only as *symbols* of the Spirit but rather as sharing in her very *being* as the Spirit is enfleshed and embodied through natural organisms and processes."[15]

Wallace is quick to acknowledge that there have been aspects of a creation-centered pneumatology in the tradition. Lifting out imagery introduced earlier in this text, Wallace lifts up the understandings of Spirit as communion, as mutuality, and as reconciler within the human community as well as the love that unites the First and Second Persons within the Trinity. Within the Greek concept of *perichoresis*, it is the Spirit who effects the mutual indwelling of the divine persons within one another. Moreover, the unitive activity of the Spirit is not only operative within the life of the Trinity, but between the Trinity and its beloved creation.

> As the Spirit exists perichoretically within the Godhead to foster communion between the divine persons, my proposal is that the Spirit also performs the role of the *vinculum caritatis* within nature in order to promote the well-being and fecundity of creation.[16]

According to Wallace, nature *enfleshes* God's sustaining love. Because of this, the Trinity is boundless love for creation and its

---

13   Wallace, "The Green Face of God," 316.

14   Wallace, "The Green Face of God," 316, emphasis in original.

15   Wallace, "The Green Face of God," 316, emphasis in original.

16   Wallace, "The Green Face of God," 317.

creatures with a "boundless passion" for the preservation, growth, and flourishing of the web of life. Revealed in the entities and processes of nature as Creator, Redeemer, and Sustainer, the Trinity itself is the basis for what Wallace terms "the greening of trinitarian theology."[17]

> The first move to an embodied doctrine of God is signaled by the inaugural hymn of Genesis where the Creator Spirit (*ruah*) breathes the world into existence and thereby enfleshes itself in the creation and maintenance of the natural order. The embodiment of the divine life in Jesus is the second move toward a nature-centered model of the Godhead. And the perichoretic union of Jesus in the Spirit—like Jesus, an earth being as well but now figured in the biblical tropes of water, dove, fire, and wind—represents the third move toward a biophilic notion of God.[18]

As one might expect, such a model of the Trinity and, more particularly, of the Spirit, is not a prominent perspective in the tradition. Although the Spirit has been recognized as Spirit of God and Spirit of creation, the emphasis has regularly fallen on the divine essence of the Spirit and the Spirit's role in salvation to the depreciation and detriment of the Spirit's biocentricity. To address the ecological crisis, however, Wallace contends that there must be a shift back to the understanding of Spirit *in* and *of* creation. It is through this revelation that "the Spirit reveals herself as a healing and subversive lifeform."[19] In the "coinherence" of the Spirit and the world of nature, the Spirit is the "interanimating force" that draws all creation into harmonious interrelationship. Wallace asserts that in such coinherence, the Spirit and nature are *inseparable*, and yet *distinguishable*. While earth and Spirit are both living realities that sustain nature's lifeforms, "Spirit and earth also possess their own distinctive identities insofar as the Spirit is the unseen power who vivifies and sustains all living things while the earth is the visible agent of the life that pulsates throughout creation."[20] In this way, Wallace proposes, the earth can be envi-

---

17   Wallace, "The Green Face of God," 318.

18   Wallace, "The Green Face of God," 318.

19   Wallace, "The Green Face of God," 318.

20   Wallace, "The Green Face of God," 319.

sioned as the body of the Spirit, who is continually enfleshed in the reality of nature. Thus, the Spirit can be said to *ensoul* the earth, as the earth is said to *enflesh* the Spirit. As the Spirit "inhabits the earth as its invisible and life giving breath," the earth is the Spirit's "outward manifestation."[21] Clearly, such proposals challenge the traditional understanding of the Divine as immutable, impassible, and self-subsistent. Moreover, such an ecological pneumatology puts the life of the Divine at risk, since "God as Spirit is vulnerable to serious loss and trauma just insofar as the earth is abused and despoiled."[22]

Is there a role that an ecological pneumatology can play in the healing of earth in response to the ecological crisis of our day? Wallace proposes that the Spirit be understood as the "wounded" or "cruciform" Spirit who, like Christ, takes upon herself "the burden of human sin and the deep ecological damage this sin has wrought in the biosphere."[23] Nonetheless, the Spirit's embodied presence in the natural world provides *hope*, according to Wallace, because that enduring presence reminds human beings of God's desire for the well-being of all creation. In a cosmological form of the paschal mystery, which is borne by the Spirit, "out of death comes life, from loss and suffering comes the possibility of hope and renewal." Wallace has this reminder for humanity:

> [To] this point the cruciform Spirit has not withdrawn her sustaining presence from the planet—a reminder to us that God is a lover of all things bodily and earthly.... May the Holy Spirit, as divine force for sustenance and renewal in all things, come into our hearts and minds and persuade us to work toward a seamless social-environmental ethic of justice toward all God's creatures.[24]

---

21   Wallace, "The Green Face of God," 320.

22   Wallace, "The Green Face of God," 320. In his article, Wallace presents a compelling example of the assault on the earth and thus on the Spirit through the scourge of environmental racism. He chronicles what effects the dumping of toxic waste in urban and rural America has had on his bioregion in the city of Chester, PA.

23   Wallace, "The Green Face of God," 326.

24   Wallace, "The Green Face of God," 327–28.

Wolfhart Pannenberg: "The Field of Force"

In his article "God as a Field of Force: Personhood and Science in Wolfhart Pannenberg's Pneumatology," theologian Timothy Harvie makes the following assertion:

> While there have been recent attempts to bring science and theology together...no systematic theologian has done so more than Wolfhart Pannenberg. Pannenberg has argued the compatibility of scientific and theological paradigms and has sought to integrate them into a mutually enhancing discourse. This is nowhere more evident than in Pannenberg's constructive account of pneumatology.[25]

Like many before and since, however, the translation of scientific concepts into theological ones—and vice versa—has proved both challenging and challenged by those who contend that such translation distorts the original meaning on both sides of the presumed equation.[26] According to theologian Wolfhart Pannenberg, this challenge can be mitigated by attending to the levels on which the dialogue takes place. "In the dialogue between theologians and scientists, it is important to be aware of the fact that such dialogue does not move on the level of scientific or religious discourse but rather on the level of philosophical reflection on both scientific terms and theories and religious doctrines."[27]

To demonstrate his assertion, Pannenberg points out that there are many philosophical notions that are utilized in both theological and scientific contexts such as causality, law, and contingency. This crossover is critical for Pannenberg, since these concepts are not only indispensable for a discussion of divine action in the world, but also

---

25   Timothy Harvie, "God as a Field of Force: Personhood and Science in Wolfhart Pannenberg's Pneumatology," *Heythrop Journal* LII (2011): 250.

26   See John C. Polkinghorne, *One World: The Interaction of Science and Theology* (Philadelphia: Templeton Foundation Press, 2007), 9, who is particularly critical of Pannenberg on such claims.

27   Wolfhart Pannenberg, "God as Spirit—and Natural Science," *Zygon* 36:4 (December 2001): 783.

for relating this divine action to scientific concepts such as space and time. Hence both science and theology can find common discourse "at some level" in the realm of philosophy, which makes the essential dialogue between them possible.[28] This is especially necessary for Pannenberg, who maintains that it is imperative to have an "empirical correlate" for the Spirit's presence and action in the material world.[29] Thus, Pannenberg poses the following questions:

> But how is the creator to be understood as active in the particularities of his creation?... And how is God's divine power related to the natural "forces" that are effective in the movements of his creatures? As these movements are taking place in space and time, God's relationship to space and time has to be clarified in such a way that his powerful presence with his creatures and their movements in space and time becomes intelligible.[30]

In response to these questions, and prompted by St. Paul's reference to God's *dynamis* or force in Romans 1:20, Pannenberg's pneumatology turns to the scientific notion of "field of force."

Pannenberg indicates the importance of recognizing that, since the third century, the understanding of God as Spirit (John 4:24) had been interpreted as *nus* or mind. This interpretation, advanced by Origen, intended to counteract the Stoic notion of *pneuma* which, while connoting air in movement or force, nonetheless had a materialist connotation. Pannenberg, however, emphasized that, in the creation story of Genesis 1, *pneuma* correlates with the Hebrew word *ruah*, meaning "wind," "storm," or "breath." Hence, "when it is said that in the beginning God's "spirit" was "moving" over the primeval waters, the image is that of a storm agitating those waters. This spirit is the source of all movement."[31] Furthermore, Biblical *pneuma* is also considered the source of life in all creatures (Genesis 2:7; Ecclesiastes 12:7). Nevertheless, while the spirit as the wind or breath of the Divine is recognized as both life and movement in Biblical understanding, "it seems a world apart from

---

28   Pannenberg, "God as Spirit," 783.

29   Pannenberg, *Toward a Theology of Nature*, 127.

30   Pannenberg, "God as Spirit," 786.

31   Pannenberg, "God as Spirit," 786.

modern science and from its ways of accounting for the movements of bodies and especially for life."[32]

So thought Pannenberg until reading an article written by historian of scientific terminology Max Jammer on the scientific concept of "field," which Jammer considered a development on the Stoic doctrine of *pneuma*. Characterized by Jammer as a "direct precursor" to the modern field concept, *pneuma* appeared to Pannenberg to be "considerably closer to the field concept of modern physics than to the Platonic idea of a divine mind or *Nus*,"[33] while still avoiding the materialist interpretation of the Stoics. The concept of field "enable[d] Pannenberg to argue empirically for the presence of nonembodied causality, which makes plausible Christian claims regarding the Spirit's presence in creation."[34] Moreover, although explicitly using a term drawn from modern physics, Pannenberg does not consider his use of the concept to be literal, but rather metaphorical.[35] Nonetheless, its metaphorical nature does not mean that it is devoid of meaning or usefulness.

> [Field] has a clear conceptual meaning in its connection with the concepts of space and time.... It is because of its connection with the concepts of space and time that a sufficiently precise theological use of the field concept is possible that is clearly distinct from its use in physics and yet related to it.[36]

To ground his perspective, Pannenberg proceeds to engage the question of how God, who is eternal, can be related to space and time, "the only basic requirements of the field concept in the General

---

32 Pannenberg, "God as Spirit," 787.

33 Pannenberg, "God as Spirit," 787.

34 Timothy Harvie, "Resurrection and Spirit: Pannenberg's Method in Two Doctrines," *Canadian Theological Review* 2:1 (2013): 11.

35 This clarification arises from the fact that Pannenberg has been criticized by John Polkinghorne as being inconsistent with the understanding of field in physics. See Polkinghorne, "Wolfhart Pannenberg's Engagement with the Natural Sciences," *Zygon* 34 (March 1999): 151–58.

36 Pannenberg, "God as Spirit," 788.

Theory of Relativity."[37] The Christian tradition has always maintained that, although infinite and eternal, God is omnipresent to the "temporal reality" of God's creatures without implying pantheism. How is this possible? Citing the work of Samuel Clarke and Immanuel Kant, Pannenberg asserts that every unit of "geometric" space implies an infinite whole of undivided space: "geometrical space that consists of parts presupposes some undivided and infinite space, because every act of composition or division already presupposes space within which the dividing or composing takes place." The same principle applies to time: "The perception of any section of time presupposes an awareness of time as an infinite whole."[38] For Pannenberg,

> The infinite space of God's immensity...and the infinite whole of simultaneous presence that is God's eternity are implicated and presupposed in our human conceptions and in our measurements of space and time. Thus God's eternity is different from the time of his creatures, but constitutive of it, and his immensity is constitutive of the space of his creatures.[39]

This conclusion makes the concept of space and time—and thus field—applicable theologically as well as scientifically. As a result, the infinite and undivided whole of God may be envisioned as an infinite field, "the field of God's spirit that constitutes and penetrates all finite fields...[and] makes intelligible how the divine Spirit works in creation through the created reality of natural fields and forces."[40] While remaining transcendent in Godself, God grants the existence of finite events and entities within the omnipresence and eternality of God. If, as demonstrated by Genesis, the divine spirit is "the creative origin of life in all its forms," then it follows that the "ecstatic openness of life to its environment and to its future corresponds to the creative activity of the divine spirit...as a dynamic field."[41] Pannenberg proceeds to

---

37   Pannenberg, "God as Spirit," 790.

38   Pannenberg, "God as Spirit," 789.

39   Pannenberg, "God as Spirit," 790.

40   Pannenberg, "God as Spirit," 790.

41   Pannenberg, "God as Spirit," 792.

explain how the Divine Spirit, coexistent, yet transcendent in terms of time and space, acts in creation through his explication of divine will. According to Pannenberg,

> [The divine will] is to be found in the experience of a reality which presses in upon us with power, which with this dynamism wants something of us, or seems to do so, even though what it wants is not very precise.... What is primary is the idea of being contacted by an unknown power which we learn to know more precisely only when we ascribe the experience to a deity that is identified by name.[42]

According to Harvie, this explanation of divine will is consistent with Pannenberg's use of the concept of field. "The divine will is effective and is able to impress itself upon the universe and upon human beings in discernible terms that are present and accessible to universal experience."[43]

Although Pannenberg's interpretation of "Spirit" as field of force demonstrates coherence with the Christian affirmation of God's presence to and activity in creation, it is nonetheless difficult to identify to whom Pannenberg is referring when he speaks of God's Spirit. If it derives from his interpretation of *pneuma* based on John 4:24, then it seems to refer not to the Third Person of the Trinity but to the essence of divine being. If it refers, rather, to the Person of the Holy Spirit, does the terminology of force, dynamics, and power connote one who is personal? In response to such questions, Pannenberg asserts that the interpretation of Spirit as field of force includes both divine being *and* divine personhood. "The person of the Holy Spirit," Pannenberg maintains, "is not himself to be understood as the field but as a unique manifestation (singularity) of the field of the divine essentiality."[44] While commentators suggest that Pannenberg's reasoning remains unclear on this point, one interpretation of Pannenberg's field of force vis-à-vis the

---

42   Wolfhart Pannenberg, *Systematic Theology 1*, trans. Geoffrey W. Bromiley (Grand Rapids, MI: Eerdmans, 1991), 381.

43   Harvie, "Resurrection and Spirit," 13.

44   Wolfhart Pannenberg, *Systematic Theology 2*, trans. Geoffrey W. Bromiley (Grand Rapids, MI: Eerdmans, 1994), 83.

Trinity might reflect the way in which Aquinas interprets the concept of *relation* in the Trinity. Aquinas asserted that Trinitarian Personhood does not consist in *having* relation among the Persons, but rather in *being* relation, which subsists in the divine essence. In a similar fashion, one might propose that Trinitarian Personhood for Pannenberg does not consist in *having* field of force among the Persons, but rather *being* field of force, which subsists in the divine essence.

Although it is clear that Pannenberg's appropriation of field of force for the presence and action of the Holy Spirit in creation has its theological and scientific shortcomings, his proposals certainly demonstrate the "creative and evocative"[45] potential that derives from an effort to engage in the dialogue between theology and science. In his proposals, Pannenberg has demonstrated that the theologian must go beyond what the scientist is able to report, since "The reality of God is a factor in defining what nature is, and to ignore this fact leaves us with something less than a fully adequate explanation of things."[46] His proposal of the Spirit of God as field of force is one attempt at such adequacy. While Pannenberg himself affirms that the concept "needs careful assessment by the theologian," it does suggest a way in which the divine presence could be conceived in the context of the natural world. As Pannenberg counsels,

> Our task as theologians is to relate to the natural sciences as they actually exist. We cannot create our own sciences. Yet we must go beyond what the sciences provide and include our understanding of God if we are properly to understand nature.[47]

Gloria L. Schaab: "The Strange Attractor"

On all levels, the sciences confirm that cosmic evolution involves organization, adaptation, and transformation of life into a kaleidoscopic diversity of forms. Throughout this process, the universe displays continuity from one life form to another because of natural laws,

---

45   Harvie, "God as a Field of Force," 257.

46   Pannenberg, *Toward a Theology of Nature*, 48.

47   Pannenberg, *Toward a Theology of Nature*, 48.

and it exhibits novelty as life forms of increasing particularity emerge in response to their environments. Scientists have pointed out that much of this creativity occurs under conditions far from equilibrium. They have found that when open and dynamic systems such as the universe undergo even infinitesimal changes, the system as a whole tends toward a new order. Moreover, it does not require epic events to trigger creativity. Rather, dynamic systems have a high sensitivity to change and respond to even small variations in their milieux to yield surprising results.

A famous example of this creativity-through-disequilibrium has come to be known as the "butterfly effect." The name comes from a paper by meteorologist Edward Lorenz entitled "Predictability: Does the Flap of a Butterfly's Wings in Brazil Set Off a Tornado in Texas?"[48] This fanciful image symbolized his theory that small changes in the conditions of an open system could have far-reaching and unpredictable consequences. In this metaphor, the flapping of the butterfly's wings signifies a small change in the conditions of the atmosphere. This change could theoretically produce a chain of events that culminates in an unforeseen outcome, such as a tornado thousands of miles away.

Lorenz made this discovery while working on the problem of weather prediction. He generated a mathematical model to forecast the weather months in advance. After running data from his model, he decided to re-examine a particular sequence. To save time, Lorenz restarted the run from the middle of the series rather than from the beginning and top in order to shorten his data input from six decimal places to just three decimal places. He entered the data from this midpoint and restarted the model. Although he expected the results from this second run to match the results from his first, he was wrong. By the end, the results bore little resemblance to those of the original cycle. Lorenz assumed that the differences in the input were inconsequential. However, shortening the data as he did was enough to produce unexpected or chaotic behavior. Scientist that he was, Lorenz retested his results and plotted the outcomes. This is the pattern that emerged.

---

48 Edward Lorenz, "Predictability: Does the Flap of a Butterfly's Wings in Brazil Set Off a Tornado in Texas?" American Association for the Advancement of Science, https://www.ias.ac.in/article/fulltext/reso/020/03/0260-0263.

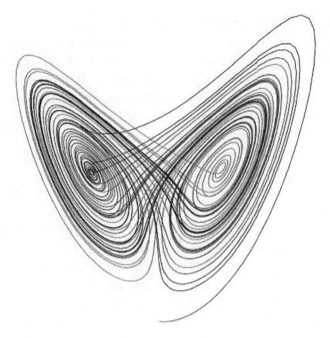

The Lorenz Attractor [49]

The appearance of this pattern revealed to Lorenz that even chaotic events have within them a subtle pattern of order. The two "wings" demonstrate that small variations in a living system can produce divergent outcomes. Nonetheless, the very formation of two "wings" demonstrates that the chaotic elements organized into a parallel pattern.

Eventually, chaos theorists termed this pattern an "attractor." An attractor is a particular state of order toward which a dynamic system tends to evolve, despite its chaotic appearance. The attractor draws chaotic events toward higher levels of organization, such that, in the midst of chaos, order emerges. The particular pattern that emerged from Lorenz's observations came to be known as the Lorenz or "butterfly attractor." The Lorenz attractor is just one example of attractors that chaos theorists have identified in dynamic systems. Scientists call these "strange attractors" because the exact nature of the attractor is not yet clearly understood. As theologian Ilia Delio, OSF, describes them: "The strange attractor is both within the system and yet different

---

49   AxiDraw Lorenz attractor (31/05/16), *Imajeenyus.com*, http://www.imajeenyus.
com/computer/20160531_axidraw_lorenz/index.shtml.

from the system's usual pattern of behavior.... It arises spontaneously and gradually lures the system into new patterns of behavior without forcing the system to change radically."[50] In systems that are dynamic, evolving, and open to change, attractors exist in unseen potential. When a confluence of chaotic events is observed over time, the strange attractor emerges as a subtle and effective principle that produces an underlying order. Because of this, the strange attractor offers an intriguing image through which to contemplate the Holy Spirit.

In an evolving universe in which natural, human, and cosmic systems are in dynamic and often chaotic flux, the strange attractor is the pattern that draws together the elements and events into coherent order in the cosmos. In like manner, the Holy Spirit is the Divine, luring the elements and events of human history toward greater harmony. In the midst of the chaos of conflict and division, self-centeredness and xenophobia, oppression and marginalization, the action of the Holy Spirit can cause a small and perhaps imperceptible change in the sensibilities of human persons, luring them beyond personal and social fragmentation toward a pattern of solidarity and community. In response to disaster and destruction, catastrophe and misfortune, the Holy Spirit reorders the remnants of these events toward patterns of healing, vitality, and new forms of life. In each of these situations and at all levels of the universe, the action of the Holy Spirit draws and integrates the random parts of cosmic life. Thus, from the seeming randomness of human and cosmic history, there emerges a graced order, a perceptible pattern that continues to draw diversity into unity, death into life, and chaos into complexity. This is the action of the Holy Spirit as the Strange Attractor.·

How might this divine Strange Attractor and the operations of the Holy Spirit be better understood? In his fanciful yet profound book *The Universe Is a Green Dragon*,[51] cosmologist Brian Swimme relates a fascinating conversation about the Strange Attractor between two speakers:

---

50   Ilia Delio, OSF, *Franciscan Prayer* (Cincinnati: St. Anthony Messenger, 2004), 41.

51   Brian Swimme, *The Universe Is a Green Dragon: A Cosmic Creation Story* (Rochester, VT: Bear & Co., 1984). The excerpts used in this section are drawn from *In Context: A Quarterly of Humane Sustainable Culture*, Context Institute; https://www.context.org/iclib/ic12/swimme/.

"Youth," who represents the human species, and "Thomas," the late cosmologist and Earth scholar Thomas Berry. In this dialogue, Youth asks Thomas about the destiny of the cosmos, and Thomas responds that Youth's destiny is "to become love in human form." Thomas goes on to explain:

> If we want to learn anything, we must start with the cosmos, the Earth, and life forms. Love begins as allurement—as attraction.... When we look at love from a cosmic perspective, we see attraction operating at every level.... Love begins there. To become fascinated, to feel allurement, is to step into a wild love affair on any level of life.[52]

What Thomas shares with Youth has profound meaning theologically. He says that the Strange Attractor, "the allurements filling the universe, of whatever complexity or order," forms a matrix of relationality and love! Is this not what Christianity says about the Holy Spirit, the love within the Trinity and between the Trinity and all creation? Without the Holy Spirit of Love, "all human groups would lose their binding energy.... Nothing left. No community of any sort. Just nothing."[53] Yet, the Holy Spirit, as the Strange Attractor, is the hidden force preventing this dissolution.

The operation of the Holy Spirit as the Strange Attractor lures the cosmos and its creatures into union, novelty, and healing in the midst of influences and dynamics that thrust them apart. Moreover, it does so in different ways and with different results at various levels of creation that it envelops. The operation of the Holy Spirit functions at each level to draw that part of the cosmos beyond that which disorders and de-energizes it into a form of life characterized by novelty, vitality, and vibrancy. However, like the Strange Attractor of chaos theory, the activity of the Holy Spirit in the cosmos is often hidden, mysterious, and undetected unless one cultivates the vision necessary to see the pattern underlying its effects.

---

52 Swimme, *The Universe is a Green Dragon*, https://www.context.org/iclib/ic12/swimme/.

53 Swimme, *The Universe is a Green Dragon*, https://www.context.org/iclib/ic12/swimme/.

Karl Rahner theorized that the Holy Spirit, whom he names as grace, draws humans into self-transcendence within themselves and in relation to other persons. He maintained that humans are existentially ordered toward "the more," always transgressing the limits of their existence toward the Infinite Horizon of God. As the impetus of such self-transcendence, the Holy Spirit draws human beings beyond the self-concern and self-preoccupation that leaves one mired in oneself. In a passage from his book *Do You Believe in God?*, Rahner gives this practical example of what such transcendence looks like:

> Have we ever made a sacrifice without receiving any thanks? Have we ever decided to do a thing simply for the sake of conscience? Have we ever tried to act purely for the love of God…when our act seemed a leap in the dark? If we can find such experiences in our life…then we have had that very experience of the Eternal.[54]

And this experience of the Eternal is the experience of the Holy Spirit.

The Holy Spirit not only orders human relationship with oneself, but also with the cosmos. The Spirit leads people to a conversion of attitudes and actions toward the cosmos and its creatures. In her essay "God's Beloved Creation," Elizabeth Johnson proposes three attitudes that manifest a renewed relation between the cosmos and humanity: the contemplative, the ascetic, and the prophetic.[55] A contemplative attitude toward creation invites persons to view the world lovingly, rather than with utilitarian arrogance. It calls one to appreciate the beauty of creation and to be awed by its mystery. An ascetic attitude encourages humans to practice discipline in using Earth's resources and to make ecologically and environmentally responsible choices. Finally, a prophetic attitude toward the cosmos recognizes the ongoing destruction of the cosmos as a sign of sinfulness and challenges persons to action for justice on behalf of Earth. This form of justice entails a movement from self-centeredness to ensure vibrant life in community for all and toward political action and structural transformation to insure the vitality of the cosmos. In an

---

54   Karl Rahner, "Do You Believe in God?" in *Foundations of Theological Study: A Sourcebook*, ed. Richard Viladesau and Mark Massa (New York: Paulist Press, 1991), 27.

55   Elizabeth A. Johnson, "God's Beloved Creation," *America* 184:13 (2001): 8–12.

evolving cosmos, "human beings cannot be separated from the earth and the material world; their transformation is part of a transformation of the world."[56] When one is drawn beyond the self-concern that serves only to de-energize and disorder, there is manifest the Strange Attractor of the Holy Spirit.

The attraction of the Holy Spirit is also effective at the level of social systems. When disorder and disintegration manifest themselves in xenophobia, exclusion, oppression, and marginalization, families, neighborhoods, communities, societies, and nations are destabilized. Nonetheless, the attraction of the Holy Spirit upon those alienated by conflict and division "changes...hearts: enemies begin to speak to one another, those who were estranged join hands in friendship, and nations seek the way of peace together." Grace is at work "when understanding puts an end to strife, when hatred is quenched by mercy, and vengeance gives way to forgiveness."[57]

This manifestation of graced transcendence at the level of social systems is often termed *liberation*. According to Latin American theologian José Comblin, grace as the power of the Holy Spirit is "holiness and justice"[58] within the community and broader culture, "the soul of the liberation movement," and "the root of the liberation of the poor."[59] In the history of the poor and oppressed, the graced action of the Holy Spirit "produces resistance, faith, hope." Moreover, in the midst of the chaos of poverty and oppression, the Spirit "is the force that awakens, animates, and maintains the struggle of the oppressed, who are victims of injustice and evil."[60] On the level of social systems, the Holy Spirit exerts a holistic effect on human existence such that the history of the Spirit's influence in cosmic life is a history of liberation.

---

56   José Comblin, "Grace," in *Mysterium Liberationis: Fundamental Concepts in Liberation Theology*, ed. Ignacio Ellacuría and Jon Sobrino (Maryknoll, NY: Orbis, 1993), 524.

57   "Eucharistic Prayers for Masses of Reconciliation II," *Basic Texts for the Roman Catholic Eucharist*, http://catholic-resources.org/ChurchDocs/EPR1-2.htm.

58   Comblin, "Grace," 526.

59   Comblin, "Grace," 530.

60   Comblin, "Grace," 530.

At all levels of life, the Holy Spirit is at work as the Strange Attractor, stirring being into becoming, luring the present toward the future, and actualizing potential within the cosmos and within each human being. As Peter Hodgson claims in his book *Winds of the Spirit*, "God, the strange attractor, is like a mighty whirlwind,"[61] drawing all things to Godself. While "not directly visible," the Holy Spirit as the Strange Attractor "appears in and through the turbulence and fluidity of countless dynamic events in natural and human history…drawing all things to itself and of sustaining and cherishing all things in relationship to it."[62] In so doing, the Holy Spirit is the power in us that "is able to accomplish far more than we ask or imagine" (Ephesians 3:20).

A CONCLUSION AND YET A LOOK AHEAD

In the beginning of this book was the Spirit in creation—the "mighty wind" who hovered over the waters (Genesis 1:2), poured out over all humankind (3:1–2), and sent forth to renew the face of the earth (Psalms 104:30)—and so it ends with that same Spirit manifest and active in the cosmos. While this particular exploration is concluding, hopefully it is yet a beginning of finding the Holy Spirit in liberating ways and in unexpected places one might not have sought before. There are few people who have captured this sense of endings as new beginnings than the poet T.S. Eliot, whose verses from "Little Gidding" provide the conclusion to this work.

> *With the drawing of this Love and the voice of this Calling*
> *We shall not cease from exploration*
> *And the end of all our exploring*
> *Will be to arrive where we started*
> *And know the place for the first time…*
> *Not known, because not looked for*
> *But heard, half-heard, in the stillness…*

---

61   Peter C. Hodgson, *Winds of the Spirit: A Constructive Christian Theology* (Louisville, KY: Westminster John Knox, 1994), 195.

62   Hodgson, *Winds of the Spirit*, 195.

Quick now, here, now, always—
...And all shall be well and
All manner of thing shall be well
When the tongues of flames are in-folded
Into the crowned knot of fire
And the fire and the rose are one.[63]

FOR REFLECTION

- This chapter proposes that dialogue is possible and even critical between theology and science to understand how God interacts with creation and its creatures. Do you agree or disagree with this proposal? How might your understanding of God be enhanced or challenged by such a dialogue?
- Which of the three images of the Spirit in creation do you find most compelling? Most engaging? Most challenging? Reflect on your response to each.
- Have you experienced the Holy Spirit as liberating at the personal, interpersonal, societal, and environmental levels suggested by Schaab? Give practical examples at each level.
- How might this be both an end and a beginning in your relationship with the Holy Spirit?

FOR FURTHER READING

Harvie, Timothy. "God as a Field of Force: Personhood and Science in Wolfhart Pannenberg's Pneumatology." *Heythrop Journal* LII (2011): 250–59.

Johnson, Elizabeth A. "God's Beloved Creation." *America* 184:13 (2001): 8–12.

Pannenberg, Wolfhart. "God as Spirit—and Natural Science." *Zygon* 36:4 (December 2001): 783–94.

Wallace, Mark I. "The Green Face of God: Christianity in an Age of Ecocide." *CrossCurrents* 50:3 (Fall 2000): 310–33.

---

63   Adapted from T.S. Eliot, "Little Gidding," http://www.columbia.edu/itc/history/winter/w3206/edit/tseliotlittlegidding.html.

INDEX